HIGHER EDUCATION
AND SDG11

HIGHER EDUCATION AND THE SUSTAINABLE DEVELOPMENT GOALS

Series Editor

Wendy Purcell

Emeritus Professor and University President Emerita, and Academic Research Scholar with Harvard University

About the Series

Higher Education and the Sustainable Development Goals is a series of 17 books that address each of the SDGs in turn specifically through the lens of higher education. Adopting a solutions-based approach, each book focuses on how higher education is advancing the delivery of sustainable development and the United Nations' global goals.

Forthcoming Volumes

Higher Education and SDG4: Quality Education edited by Tawana Kupe

Higher Education and SDG16: Peace, Justice and Strong Institutions edited by Sarah E. Mendelson

Higher Education and SDG10: Reduced Inequalities edited by Priya Grover, Nidhi Phutela, and Pragya Singh

Higher Education and the Sustainable Development Goals

HIGHER EDUCATION AND SDG11

Sustainable Cities and Communities

EDITED BY

JULIO LUMBRERAS
Universidad Politécnica de Madrid (UPM),
Spain

AND

JAIME MORENO-SERNA
Universidad Politécnica de Madrid (UPM),
Spain

United Kingdom – North America – Japan – India
Malaysia – China

Emerald Publishing Limited
Emerald Publishing, Floor 5, Northspring, 21-23 Wellington Street, Leeds LS1 4DL.

First edition 2025

Editorial matter and selection © 2025 Julio Lumbreras and
Jaime Moreno-Serna.
Individual chapters © 2025 The authors.
Published under exclusive licence by Emerald Publishing Limited.

Reprints and permissions service
Contact: www.copyright.com

No part of this book may be reproduced, stored in a retrieval system, transmitted in any form or by any means electronic, mechanical, photocopying, recording or otherwise without either the prior written permission of the publisher or a licence permitting restricted copying issued in the UK by The Copyright Licensing Agency and in the USA by The Copyright Clearance Center. No responsibility is accepted for the accuracy of information contained in the text, illustrations or advertisements. The opinions expressed in these chapters are not necessarily those of the Author or the publisher.

British Library Cataloguing in Publication Data
A catalogue record for this book is available from the British Library

ISBN: 978-1-83797-423-8 (Print)
ISBN: 978-1-83797-420-7 (Online)
ISBN: 978-1-83797-422-1 (Epub)

INVESTOR IN PEOPLE

CONTENTS

Series Editor Preface   vii

Acknowledgments   xi

1. Introduction   1
   Julio Lumbreras and Jaime Moreno-Serna

2. Transdisciplinary Research and Education to Increase the Capacity for Governing Urban Climate Transitions   9
   Harald Rohracher and Olga Kordas

3. Why Citystudio, Why Now?   27
   Duane Elverum, Alix Linaker and Marga Pacis

4. Prioritizing Principles of Justice and Collaborative Research in an African Higher Education Institution in Order to Advance Urban Sustainability: The Urban Futures Centre (Durban University of Technology) in South Africa   41
   Jennifer Houghton and Bakhetsile Mangena

5. Universidad de los Andes and Its Contribution to Bogota in the Achievement of the 2030 Agenda   63
   Juan Camilo Cardenas, Manuela Navarrete, Carla Panyella and Mónica Pinilla-Roncancio

6. The Role of Higher Education Institutions in Urban Climate Transformation   91
   John Cleveland and Azanta Thakur

7 Building A City–University Partnership for Accelerating
  Urban Climate Neutrality: The Case of València (Spain)   113
  Jordi Peris Blanes, Oksana Udovyk, Fermín Cerezo,
  Guillermo Palau, Iván Cuesta, Dionisio Ortiz Miranda,
  Jose Luis Alapont, Débora Domingo, Carla Montagud,
  Ana Escario Chust, Sergio Segura Calero and
  Pablo Aranguiz Mesias

8 National Platforms to Transform Cities Using Collective
  Experimentation and Scale: The Case of Sweden
  and Spain   145
  Jaime Moreno-Serna, Olga Kordas, Julio Lumbreras,
  Åsa Minoz, Nayla Saniour and Harald Rohracher

About the Editors   159
About the Contributors   161

SERIES EDITOR PREFACE
Professor Wendy Purcell, PhD FRSA

Higher education (HE) contributes materially to the delivery of the Sustainable Development Goals (SDGs). Through high quality teaching and learning, HE supports the development of responsible citizens as scholars, leaders, entrepreneurs, and professionals. Universities and colleges undertake curiosity-driven and socially impactful research to help advance knowledge frontiers and find solutions for the world's most pressing issues. Higher education institutions (HEIs) are also active in civic and community settings, often as anchor institutions. Nevertheless, given the fierce urgency of (un)sustainable development, the climate crisis, and widening inequity within countries and across the globe, HE needs to do more and go faster. For HE to deliver fully against the SDGs, it needs to adapt to this shared global agenda and embrace transformative change.

This book series focuses on the role of HE in advancing the SDGs, identifying some actionable and scalable initiatives, and pointing to opportunities ahead. In sharing the ways and means universities and colleges across the world are engaging with the SDGs, the series seeks to both inspire and enable those in the HE sector and stakeholders beyond to transform what they do and how they do it and thereby hasten progress toward Agenda 2030. Insights gleaned from relevant case studies, reflective accounts, and student stories can help the HE sector both deepen and accelerate its engagement with the SDGs. Each book seeks to capture examples of how HEIs are innovating to deliver their academic mission *and* progress the SDG concerned. Illustrating the work of students, that is undertaken by faculty and staff of the institution and conducted with other stakeholders and partners, positions HE as a change agent operating at a systems level to help create a world that leaves no one behind.

Taking up this global challenge, SDG11 "Sustainable Cities and Communities" calls on us to "Make cities inclusive, safe, resilient and sustainable." Bringing key assets of curiosity and the pursuit of knowledge and its application to partners seeking solutions and driving innovation, universities and colleges operate in both local and global networks. In cities, by enabling talent to express itself in our society and help realize human potential, HEIs connect the worlds of learning, work, and entrepreneurship in support of more sustainable economic growth. As place-makers, HEIs use their convening power to draw stakeholders around a problem in support of the adaptive change needed to tackle the challenges of sustainable development such as climate change and the transition to net zero.

This book on HE and SDG11 highlights the work of universities and colleges on sustainable cities and communities with examples drawn from multistakeholder ventures focused on urban transformation. A central theme is the way trustful partnerships with equity-minded leaders are created and sustained by HEIs working with a range of city and community actors from business, public sector city officials, and political leaders to foster resilience, adaptation, and a just transition. Academic knowledge comes together with the practical insights and lived experience of those in cities to advance sustainable development and new urban governance models. Many of these examples are in essence a "living lab," with real-world problems being the education space in which new pedagogies and ways of working emerge through radical collaboration with those outside the academy. In this way, the campus and city together become a shared community space for experimentation, innovation, and socio-technical actions in pursuit of more sustainable urban futures and an improved quality of life for all.

Health of people, planet, and shared prosperity rely upon the full participation of HE with universities and colleges in turn needing to pursue greater engagement with the SDGs – not least to reduce their own environmental footprint and become more equitable. As organizations that have stood for many centuries in some cases, this demands that they adapt to new models of learning, research partnerships, and leadership and governance frameworks to accelerate progress on delivering the SDGs. Immersive engagement with the SDGs can catalyze pedagogic innovation, serve to refresh curricula, and stimulate new program development. It can also open new avenues for research, attract new sources of funding, and energize people to deliver on the academic mission. Sustainability is a goal for today and sustainable development an organizing principle. HEIs can play a critical role in developing new systemic and transformative solutions through interdisciplinary and multi-stakeholder collaboration and a purposeful focus on the SDGs. This book illustrates this approach as it relates to HE and SDG11 calling for systems-based urban action and universities and colleges that are more connected to the cities and communities they serve locally and globally.

ACKNOWLEDGMENTS

Primarily, we extend tremendous gratitude to the authors of this book for investing their time in sharing their experiences and insights with the wider higher education community, and for their inspiration to transform our cities through transdisciplinary research and education, making our world a better place.

To Prof. Purcell and the team at Emerald, for your continuous support, patience, and leadership.

To our colleagues and friends at the UPM Innovation Center on Technologies for Human Development (itdUPM), who are always supportive and spend their energy on creating the conditions to grow and flourish. And to our colleagues at the EU Cities Mission, who are leading the work to transform 112 European cities to become more sustainable, safer, greener, healthier, and inclusive. This effort will drive the transformation of the continent in the coming years. All stakeholders engaged in the Cities Mission (public governments, private companies, academia, and civil society) are making the difference to create value through a just society.

1

INTRODUCTION

Julio Lumbreras and
Jaime Moreno-Serna

Universidad Politécnica de Madrid, UPM, Spain

We have already passed half of the way to meet the Sustainable Development Goals (SDGs). The 2030 Agenda is a comprehensive and very ambitious goal for us as humanity. However, we also know that it is not a will, but a must. According to science, if we don't act to transform our society, we will likely compromise the future of human life on the Earth, both from a social and environmental standpoint. Therefore, there is a need for urgent and accelerated transformation of our societal model.

Cities play a fundamental role in this transformation. More than half of world's population lives in cities, and the United Nations projections show that this percentage would increase to 68% in 2050.[1] Moreover, cities are currently responsible for 65% of total global energy consumption and more than 70% of CO_2 emissions.[2] Cities also act as centers for innovation as social, technological, and political innovations easily meet people and are closely connected to their needs. Even more, they are experimentation hubs that can drive the implementation of the SDGs. Therefore, cities are critical to transform our society.

This urban transformation is very much needed to transform our society, but it is also relevant to solve urban unsustainability. There are significant social, environmental, and economical problems in cities. Some of the main problems are: social inequality between neighborhoods, racial problems, lack of access to adequate, safe, and affordable housing, poor air quality, lack of safely managed drinking water, lack of access to electricity or modern fuels, loss of biodiversity, noise pollution, etc. So cities also need a profound transformation to become more sustainable, evolving to become healthier, greener, more inclusive, safer, with more opportunities, more jobs, and access to affordable and high quality services. At the end of the day, cities should be places where citizens have a better quality of life.

However, this transformation could not be done through punctual, disconnected, and incremental changes. There is a need for a systemic transformation in cities. And the higher education sector could and should play a central role for this sustainable transition. In particular:

- Most of the universities are urban, and they act as cities within cities.
- They can align research to solve urban problems.
- They educate students who could transform cities in the future, and they can also train other citizens through their life-long learning process.
- They can act as test beds showcasing an alternative way of managing resources and offering services and experimenting new technological and governance systems in their campuses.
- They can convene different stakeholders to find systemic solutions using the neutral and legitimate role they have.

This book shows some examples of how universities can play this distinctive role with an innovative approach to the traditional triple HE mission:

- *Research*: transdisciplinary research with municipalities, using social and environmental justice across research actions.

- *Education*: aligning capstones and master thesis to solve urban problems.

- *Societal impact*: through a profound collaboration with the city to transform it, fostering radical collaboration between different cities from the same context.

In particular, the second chapter presents how collaborative transdisciplinary research and education between universities and municipal partners can enhance cities' transformative capacities to address major societal challenges like climate change. Transformative change in urban governance demands new organizational structures, competencies, and administrative processes, as current structures often lack adequacy for addressing the systemic nature, uncertainty, and complexity of sustainability challenges. Collaborative efforts between universities and the public sector can deepen our understanding of new governance strategies for transformative change while enhancing our collective ability to implement them. Examples of such collaborations are discussed, focusing on key aspects of urban transformative capacities such as understanding systemic change, adopting experimental governance approaches, integrating initiatives, establishing processes for reflective monitoring and learning, and integrating policy areas like climate and social policy.

The third chapter explains the initiative called CityStudio, which is an adaptable, plug and play model that helps global cities create a permanent partnership with local HEIs for collaboration, research, projects, and mutual benefit. CityStudio assists cities to identify and distribute priority needs to local HEIs universities, providing increased capacity for cities and work-integrated learning opportunities for students on real-world projects. By providing students with the opportunity to work on projects related to this goal, CityStudio helps to cultivate the next generation of urban leaders and innovators who are committed to building more sustainable and equitable cities. CityStudio also provides students with resources and support to help them develop their own ideas and projects. For example, students may have access to mentorship and coaching from city staff and community leaders, as well as funding to help bring their projects to life. Since launching, there are 14 CityStudios across the globe that has cumulatively seen over 703 city staff work with 12,000 students on 2,615 projects, contributing over 300,000 student hours to local civic priorities.[3] Students at CityStudio have created community gardens, pop-up parks, street furniture, murals, and events. They have also analyzed every kilometer of the bike path, mapped food deserts, proposed land use policy, counted intertidal species as well as dog waste in parks, Students have improved settlement services, developed community skill shares, and tested beach-front water quality. They have presented their work to City council to show how these experiments and reversible trials – designed and implemented by students, instructors, and city staff – improve our city and our lives.

The fourth chapter delves into the pivotal role of higher education institutions (HEIs), with a focus on the Urban Futures Centre at the Durban University of Technology in South Africa, in driving sustainable development agendas, particularly within the context of rapidly growing African cities facing sustainability challenges. Through a lens of social and environmental justice, HEIs like the Urban Futures Centre employ collaborative, interdisciplinary, and applied methodologies to tackle pressing urban issues, including marine resource management, harm reduction for homeless drug users, and urban flooding. By integrating SDG concepts into their teaching, research, and campus operations, HEIs not only advance sustainability agendas but also foster transformative learning and action. Moreover, their direct engagement with communities, stakeholders, and the diverse urban realities across Africa underscores the importance of flexible, context-sensitive approaches to address pressing development needs and promote inclusive, resilient, and sustainable urban futures on the continent.

The fifth chapter shows how universities can play an important role in decarbonizing cities and tackle inequalities in urban settings. Both challenges are particularly critical in Latin America and the Caribbean region where demographic transition toward urban areas and the persistent inequalities have increased the ecological footprint of human activities and the economy in general. The chapter discusses how universities can contribute in a multifaceted manner to the achievement of SDG11, its specific targets, and explore the synergies between SDG11 and other important SDGs in the Latin American and the Caribbean region. The chapter presents the experience of the Center of the Sustainable Development Goals for Latin America and the Caribbean (CODS) in monitoring the progress in the achievement of the SDGs in the region. In addition, the trajectory of the Universidad de los Andes in Colombia is used to illustrate the challenges and the possibilities for a HEI in contributing to moving toward a more sustainable urban setting. These strategies include not only education and research, but also how it has intervened in the immediate neighborhood of the campus, the close ties with the city administration over decades, and close interactions with the private sector at the local and national levels.

The sixth chapter focuses on the unique role the HEIs can play in informing, facilitating, and accelerating the transformation that cities need to accomplish their climate goals for net zero emissions and long-term resilience. Cities will need to radically transform their core urban systems of transportation, energy, waste, buildings, and stormwater management, among others. Multiple billions of dollars will have to be invested by the public and private sectors, and governance structures for planning, regulation and decision-making will need to be restructured to rapidly adapt to changing climate demands. In this sense, High-Ed research knowledge can inform investments and regulatory decision-making; their students can provide the critical skills needed by private and public stakeholders to support implementation; their campuses can act as "living labs" to test out innovative climate solutions; and their political influence can help inform and advance needed public policy changes. The chapter exemplifies this role explaining the Boston Green Ribbon Commission (GRC) which is a CEO network whose mission is to accelerate the implementation of the City's Climate Action Plan by convening, organizing, and enabling leaders from Boston's key sectors. The case is particularly relevant, as Boston and its metro surroundings have one of the highest concentrations of HEIs in the world. The chapter also shares the lessons learned from the GRC and the HEWG on how HEIs can help convene key stakeholders to accelerate the urban transformation needed to achieve ambitious climate goals.

The seventh chapter shows the example of a city–university partnership (CUP), in Valencia, Spain. CUPs are emerging and dynamic collaborations addressing urban challenges in various cities. The Valencian CUP functions as a multi-faceted entity, serving as a knowledge powerhouse, innovation catalyst in urban policies, and a vital educational space. The chapter unfolds various dimensions of the CUP's impact, emphasizing its contributions to the city's development model, innovation in urban policies, and transdisciplinary education. Examining collaborations and transformations leading to CUP creation and effective functioning through the multi-level perspective (MLP) framework illuminates a complexity of the CUP in Valencia. It also highlights the catalytic role of the EU Cities Mission in shaping CUP creation. The CUP in Valencia stands as a beacon of inspiration and a blueprint for global urban centers navigating the path toward climate neutrality.

The final chapter presents the role of universities in creating National Platforms for Cities, such as Viable Cities and citiES 2030 in Sweden and Spain respectively. These platforms signify a shift toward deep collaboration and collective action among cities to achieve ambitious sustainability goals, particularly in the context of the EU's mission to achieve 100 climate-neutral cities by 2030.[4] They serve as intermediaries fostering multi-level and multi-stakeholder collaborations, promoting cross-city interactions, aligning national and European initiatives, and co-creating innovative practices for climate urban transitions. Universities play a crucial role in initiating and sustaining these platforms, leveraging their neutrality, legitimacy, and knowledge capabilities to strengthen collaborative efforts and drive transformative actions. By serving as unifying agents, providing interdisciplinary expertise, offering educational methodologies, and facilitating city-driven initiatives, universities contribute to the development and implementation of ambitious commitments, capability building, and transformative actions within these national platforms. Moreover, these platforms embody systemic approaches, facilitating innovative governance tools and programs that address regulatory challenges, enhance energy efficiency, and strengthen local capacities, while also providing opportunities for universities to engage in purpose-driven research and training programs aligned with societal needs.

In summary, the cases explored reveal the diversity of approaches and strategies that HEIs can develop to contribute to the sustainable transformation of our cities. Each context presents its own challenges and opportunities, but the importance of the academic community assuming a more committed role in promoting significant changes in our immediate environments is evident. As we progress in this book, we will delve into the depths of each experience, extracting valuable lessons that will hopefully inspire us to forge a more inclusive, sustainable, and prosperous urban future for all.

NOTES

1. UN Department of Economic and Social Affairs, 2018. More info at: https://www.un.org/uk/desa/68-world-population-projected-live-urban-areas-2050-says-un and https://population.un.org/wup/?_gl=1*g5xfjv*_ga*NTY1NDA3NDM4LjE3MTMxMjk5OTE.*_ga_TK9BQL5X7Z*MTcxMzEyOTk5MC4xLjEuMTcxMzEzMDA3MC4wLjAuMA.

2. 100 climate-neutral cities by 2030 – by and for the citizens (mission board report). European Commission, 2021. Available here: https://op.europa.eu/en/web/eu-law-and-publications/publication-detail/-/publication/82f1df57-b68b-11ea-bb7a-01aa75ed71a1.

3. CityStudio Webpage: https://citystudioglobal.com/.

4. EC Cities Mission. All information available at: https://research-and-innovation.ec.europa.eu/funding/funding-opportunities/funding-programmes-and-open-calls/horizon-europe/eu-missions-horizon-europe/climate-neutral-and-smart-cities_en.

2

TRANSDISCIPLINARY RESEARCH AND EDUCATION TO INCREASE THE CAPACITY FOR GOVERNING URBAN CLIMATE TRANSITIONS

Harald Rohracher[a] and Olga Kordas[b]

[a]*Department of Thematic Studies – Technology and Social Change, Linköping University, Linköping, Sweden*
[b]*KTH Royal Institute of Technology, Centre for Sustainable Built Environment, Strategic Innovation Programme Viable Cities, Stockholm, Sweden*

ABSTRACT

In this chapter, the authors present an argument and illustrations for how transdisciplinary research and education in close collaboration between universities and non-academic partners in municipalities can contribute to building transformative capacities in cities to tackle grand societal challenges such as climate change. Governing transformative change requires new types of capacities and capabilities of the public sector such as new organizational structures, competencies, and administrative rules and processes. Current urban governance structures often are not adequate to deal with the type of challenges urban sustainability transitions pose: the systemic nature of the problems, the absence of clearly defined solutions in combination with a high level of uncertainty about goals and pathways to reach them, the long-time-perspective and complexity of change processes which need to involve a broad range of actors and stakeholders, or the need to work across different sectors and policy fields. Boundary-crossing research and education activities between universities and the public sector can simultaneously enhance our understanding of new governance strategies for transformative change and our joint capacity to implement them. In this chapter, the authors draw on examples of such collaborations which are dealing with key elements of urban transformative capacities such as a better understanding of systemic dimensions of change, a shift to experimental governance approaches, and at the same time systemic integration of experiments and initiatives, the development of processes for reflexive monitoring and learning, or the need to integrate policy areas such as climate and social policy.

Keywords: Climate-neutral cities; transdisciplinary research; transition governance; knowledge co-creation; monitoring and evaluation; transformative planning

BUILDING CAPACITIES FOR URBAN CLIMATE TRANSITION

Cities have become one of the crucial arenas in our fight against the climate crises. They are on the one hand major emitters of greenhouse gases due to rapid growth and urbanization, but also as drivers of consumption-oriented lifestyles and the environmental loads coming along with this. At the same time, cities worldwide are highly exposed to the consequences of climate change and suffer the consequences of urban heat islands, traffic congestions, air pollution, or rising sea levels. On the other hand, cities are hotbeds for all kinds of innovation, experimentation, and social transformation. As centers of knowledge production and cultural diversity, due to the proximity and density of actors and actor networks, but also because of the interwovenness of urban techno-structures (Rohracher & Ornetzeder, 2019), they are as much part of the problem as they are part of the answer of developing a more sustainable society and economy. As Elmqvist et al. (2019, p. 267) put it: "We have entered the urban century and addressing a broad suite of sustainability challenges in urban areas is increasingly key for our chances to transform the entire planet towards sustainability."

Indeed, many of the sustainability challenges our cities and societies are facing today require fundamental transformations in the way we live, work, consume, and organize our economies. Such change processes are systemic and require a broad perspective on the interrelations of institutions, technologies, and social practices; they are intersectoral and multi-actor; they are long-term despite their urgency; and they constitute wicked problems, with no clear solutions and shifting problem understandings. A growing field of interdisciplinary social science research on "sustainability transitions" deals with the dynamics and governance of such transformative, systemic, socio-technical change processes toward sustainability (Geels, 2005; Köhler et al., 2019; Truffer et al., 2022). Contributing to such a goal requires a sound understanding of the socio-technical relations that create the stable structures characteristic of our current regimes of mobility, energy or food production, but also a better understanding of the dynamics of systemic change and of opportunities for intervening in the creation of pathways toward greater sustainability. Cities are exceptional places to govern transformative change within a broader multi-level governance context: they are close to citizens and other urban actors, they are creative milieus with a high concentration of start-ups and social movements, and they command substantial "soft governance power" to initiate and facilitate change processes (Bulkeley & Castán Broto, 2013). This role of cities in sustainability transitions has been increasingly recognized in the transition studies literature (Bulkeley et al., 2011; Frantzeskaki et al., 2017; Rohracher & Späth, 2014; Romero-Lankao et al., 2018; Torrens et al., 2021).

A key strategy within this context has been the support and protection of emerging niches where new technical solutions can be tested and further developed in a context of use and social embedding (Smith & Raven, 2012). Along these lines of emerging niches as testbeds, much research has focused on designing and implementing socio-technical experiments where not only new technologies, but whole socio-technical arrangements such as car-free city districts are at stake (Engels et al., 2019; Karvonen & van Heur, 2014). Particularly cities are seen as preferred places for such experimental approaches to build momentum for change (Evans et al., 2016; Mukhtar-Landgren et al., 2019) and contexts for urban testbeds and living labs (Bulkeley et al., 2019). Such approaches also became important elements of a new paradigm of transformative innovation policy (Schot & Steinmueller, 2018) or mission-oriented policies (Mazzucato, 2018) as an answer to new societal challenges.

Despite this potentially outstanding role of cities in the transition of our societies and economies toward sustainability, many cities lack the capacity to govern and drive such processes of transformative change (Castán Broto et al., 2019). The specific character of societal challenges – their long-term orientation far beyond election cycles and the need to work with long-term visions, their systemic complexity and interrelatedness and the need for a holistic perspective, their dependence on the engagement and collaboration of a broad range of actors also beyond the municipal administration, their relation to social values leading to conflicts and controversies, as well as the uncertainty about what works and what does not and the need to constantly test, evaluate, and adapt – requires a whole new set of organizational structures, competences, and governance approaches in cities. Based on these challenges, a framework for urban transformative capacities has been suggested (Wolfram, 2016; Wolfram et al., 2019) which comprises a variety of components: an inclusive and multi-form governance which accounts for diversity; transformative leadership; empowered communities of practice; systems analysis to understand dynamics of change; sustainability foresight and other forms of visioning processes; experimentation with novel solutions; the embedding of effective sustainability innovations; as well as reflexivity and social learning. Commanding effective transition governance capacities means pushing beyond many of the tools and instruments which have become widely accepted in the transition discussion (Hölscher et al., 2019), that is, translating long-term and systemic visions into institutional change and new financial instruments, moving beyond decentralized and bottom-up "coalitions of the willing" and develop effective forms of coordination and collaboration, as well as moving beyond experimentation and develop new ways of connecting and integrating the variety of existing pilot projects and initiatives. Hestad et al. (2021) and Peris-Blanes et al. (2022) have applied and operationalized such a capacity framework for the local contexts of Valencia and Barcelona and highlighted the importance of specific types of actors such as local governments, sustainability-oriented hybrid organizations, or local social movements for building transformative capacities.

THE CONTRIBUTION OF HIGHER EDUCATION INSTITUTIONS TO URBAN SUSTAINABILITY TRANSITIONS

This turn of policy and innovation efforts toward long-term and fundamental societal challenges has not left the science system untouched. Many researchers and departments at universities have increasingly oriented their research toward societal problems. This move poses various epistemological challenges and requires a much more interdisciplinary organization of research, an increased collaboration with non-academic actors, and new forms of knowledge integration. Science and society have become "transgressive arenas" which are co-mingling and become subject to the same co-evolutionary trends (Nowotny et al., 2001). These epistemic shifts have been discussed in different concepts such as "mode 2 science" (Gibbons et al., 1994) which is characterized by knowledge production in the context of application, transdisciplinarity, a higher degree of heterogeneity and organizational diversity as well as emphasis on social accountability and reflexivity, post-academic science (Ziman, 1996), post-normal science (Ravetz, 2011), or the triple helix model (Etzkowitz & Leydesdorff, 2000) with a focus on university–industry–government relations which has meanwhile been extended to quadruple helix constellations including civil society (McAdam & Debackere, 2018). Dealing with complex societal problems requires the integration of knowledge from different disciplines, the cooperation with societal stakeholders, and new interfaces between science and policy, as discussed in the literature on transdisciplinarity (Klein, 2014; Renn, 2021).

Of particular importance in this research process is the development of a joint problem framing between societal and academic actors and the integration of knowledge produced in the interdisciplinary research process with societal practice (Jahn et al., 2012). Organizationally this demands the creation of new "trading zones" between academia and extra-scientific partners, where knowledge and experiences can be exchanged and boundary work is performed to coproduce answers to societal needs (Felt et al., 2016). Often such connecting activities between science and societal actors are promoted and developed by different kinds of intermediary organizations (Kivimaa et al., 2019). Even universities can take on such an intermediary role and engage in co-creation activities for sustainability together with public, economic, and civil society actors (Trencher et al., 2014). Universities and transdisciplinary research units are thus in an excellent position to participate in co-creation arenas together with cities and contribute to the building of urban capacities for dealing with climate change. The remaining part of this chapter will zoom in on some examples of such a collaboration of academia and municipalities in Sweden.

Viable Cities: A Program Facilitating Climate-neutral Cities in Sweden

A central node in these developments in Sweden is the strategic innovation program "Viable Cities" which acts as an intermediary between public authorities, academia, business, civil society, and municipalities.[1] The program is co-funded by Sweden's innovation agency Vinnova, the Swedish Energy Agency, and the Swedish sustainability research council Formas. The program has a budget of 100 million euros over 12 years (2017–2030) to invest in research and innovation aiming at just transition to post-carbon cities. After around six years of activity, a project portfolio has been built up gathering more than 200 actors ranging from big cities, universities, and companies to eco-villages, start-ups, and non-governmental organizations. Its mission is seen as a manifestation of the necessary scale and scope of the ambition to meet the grand challenges of combating climate change, ecological regeneration, and unlocking the full potential of citizens in the age of digitalization and automation. The aim is to provide strategic intelligence for orchestrating systemic urban transformation, support actions to reframe societal institutions for a more equitable and circular economy, contribute to responsible and ground-breaking technological development as well as behavioral shifts required for a sustainable and just low-carbon economy and society. In 2018, Viable Cities started a mission-oriented program for "Climate-neutral Cities 2030" where meanwhile 23 Swedish municipalities took the lead in the climate transition. Collaborations between municipalities, academia, and other stakeholders were a precondition for the participation in this program. Learning between all the involved partners is organized through a Transition Lab which facilitates system transitions toward climate-neutral inclusive cities through co-creating mission arenas for the mobilization of societal actors, through developing compelling and inclusive narratives framed as meaningful outcomes of sustainability and climate transitions for both citizens and cities, through implementing a portfolio approach and leverage on synergies, creating mechanisms for regulatory and organizational change to facilitate outcome-based policy and practice, and driving institutional learning through evaluation, benchmarking, and reflexivity. Much in line with our discussion above, Viable Cities is facilitating the build-up of transition capacities, not least by connecting cities with universities and other actors.

Building Capacities for Monitoring, Evaluation, and Learning

A first example of how transdisciplinary research in collaboration with municipalities can contribute to transformative capacities is recent research in the context of Viable Cities aiming at developing new structures for the monitoring and evaluating transformative change. Traditional strategies of evaluating policy programs or projects are mostly ex post and outcome-oriented, that is, assessing the results and impacts of a project. Transformative and mission-oriented programs such as the transition to climate-neutral cities or the Sustainable Development Goals (SDGs) aim at much longer, sometimes generational, changes which make an ex post evaluation almost impossible. Moreover, they are only one of many interventions which makes it difficult to attribute impacts in hindsight to specific projects. Not least, such programs and goals deal with wicked problems where no clear and widely agreed solutions exist which makes it difficult to define appropriate criteria for success. Monitoring and evaluating such transformative policies requires new approaches which are formative and development-oriented, contributing to learning processes of all actors involved (Haddad & Bergek, 2023; Molas-Gallart et al., 2021). Much of this work focuses on developing new processes and approaches to evaluation and identifying social impacts, learning, and other key dimensions of transformation. Also, the discussion about appropriate indicators for assessing ongoing transformation processes is only at the beginning. A problem of many existing indicator systems is that their practical relevance and impact on policymaking is very limited (Lyytimäki, 2019). They often exclusively focus on numeric indicators and on measuring what is easily measurable (Yli-Viikari, 2009). Moreover, studies of indicator systems also point to the politics behind such indicators, the way they are performative and shape pathways of change, maintain or change power relations and economic interests, how they make certain aspects visible while they hide other dimensions from sight and political awareness (Dunlop & Völker, 2023). Indicator systems are a political terrain, they are a space where social futures are negotiated and shaped (Völker et al., 2020).

As one of the first steps in the Viable Cities Transition Lab,[2] a workshop has been convened with stakeholders from Viable Cities to explore approaches to "monitor transformative change." In total, the workshop hosted 68 participants and was held during a one-day event in October 2019 in Stockholm, Sweden. The majority of the participants came from the academic and local government sectors. This workshop was the starting point of a still ongoing endeavor for developing reflexive and learning-oriented monitoring processes and appropriate transformative indicator for Swedish cities aiming at climate neutrality. Making such processes legible and understandable is a precondition for making them governable and is thus a crucial capacity for cities to be able to govern their transformation process. Understanding such indicator systems as "sites of social imagination" where cities negotiate and imagine sustainable futures (Völker et al., 2020), means that they cannot be developed by research alone but require a truly transdisciplinary co-creation process. At the same time, research input is essential to make use of the increasing knowledge base about the dynamics of transformative change.

A more practical application of this city–academia collaboration about monitoring change is an empirical project following up on the development of a sustainable city district, Vallastaden, in the city of Linköping which is part of the Climate-neutral Cities 2030 program. Academic research helps to unpack the innovation journey leading to the city district and the experiences made during planning and implementation. This is then used as a basis for the city administration to reflect on how these insights can be used in the further planning and development process. Such considerations have rarely been made in the city in a more systematic fashion and aimed at further process improvement. In this sense, this is an example of a transdisciplinary collaboration process in practice where universities become part of a joint arena of work toward sustainable cities and SDG11.

A Transdisciplinary Research School on Just Transitions

A further example of transdisciplinary research and collaboration on urban climate transitions is a new PhD research school on "Just Transitions," funded by the Swedish sustainability research council Formas.[3] Universities in Gothenburg and Linköping team up with both cities and the respective regions to ask how questions of justice and equality can best be integrated into urban climate transition governance and how urban capacities can be built to deal with such questions. Not only does this research school bring together departments which have been working separately with questions of justice and social work on the one side, and transformative change, interactive design, and human ecology on the other, but each of the current seven PhD projects is deeply connected to urban and regional policy and administration. Each PhD student has a practice supervisor from one of the cities and is embedded in practice contexts, for example, by having a workplace both at the university and the urban or regional administration and spending at least some of their PhD time directly in these practice contexts. Moreover, academic and practice supervisors together with the PhD students closely collaborate in defining problems in a way which is relevant to urban administrative and governance practice and the practical challenges the governance of climate transitions is facing, and which at the same time are linked to current academic discourses and research. At the time of writing, transdisciplinary research projects are designed in each of the municipalities which eventually will become the basis for PhD theses, but also serve as an input into further strategy development on just transitions in the respective cities. PhD students, supervisors, and practitioners participate together in courses and seminars which deal with conflicts and dilemmas in urban planning and decision-making for just climate transitions; explore justice as a situated, relational, and spatial practice with distributive, procedural, and recognitional dimensions; develop transdisciplinary, boundary-spanning methods for research and transformation; and build capacities and competences for just climate transitions.

The research school is in itself a social experiment which tests how a PhD education can be organized in a transdisciplinary and problem-oriented way in collaboration between academia and urban and regional practitioners. In line with this experimental approach, a formative evaluation process has been initiated which will provide regular opportunities to take stock of what has already been achieved and reflect on the ongoing process. Regular "transdisciplinary learning sessions" will make it possible to adapt the research school processes and improve problem-oriented collaboration capacities between researchers and practitioners. One element of capacity building which has become visible in the early phases of the research school is the adjustment of mutual expectations – the competence needed at the side of urban and regional practitioners to better understand which kind of problems and solutions are accessible for research (in contrast to, e.g., consultancy), but also the competence from universities and researchers to collaboratively develop problems and design research. The ambition is to extend the research school in the longer term into a national platform where universities and cities collaborate in PhD education related to the urban climate transition.

Re-organizing Planning Education for Transformative Change

A final and again different example of how higher education institutions can contribute to building urban transformative capacities toward climate neutrality and sustainability is a project at Linköping University which spans undergraduate and graduate programs in urban and regional planning at Swedish universities and asks how planning education can adapt to the challenges of transformative change. Traditional urban planning has long followed a "public sector logic" which aims at sustaining democratic legitimacy and prioritizes order, control, and stability, in contrast to an experimental planning logic which is more adequate for transformative change and is characterized by the collaborative, testing, learning, and innovative structure of urban experimentation (Berglund-Snodgrass & Mukhtar-Landgren, 2020). Also, Wolfram et al. (2019) point out that challenging and reinventing urban planning is a key arena for developing urban transformative capacities. Urban planning has a major potential as a "cross-sector, multi-scalar, and place-based action domain, linked to an intrinsic aspiration for resolving goal conflicts by applying 'comprehensive' approaches, and the possibility to draw in diverse resources, skills, and competencies." (Wolfram et al., 2019, p. 444). Swedish planning education (which is offered at 12 universities) has however not yet reacted sufficiently to these new demands and roles of planning in urban transition processes. In collaboration with urban planning practitioners and those responsible for planning education at universities, new skills, competences, and knowledge for transformative urban planning are identified. Planning education needs to strengthen planners' skills and competences in managing uncertainties in transition processes (working with long-term visions and directionality of change, including experimental approaches), engage in multi-actor collaborations (creating platforms and facilitating interaction and collaboration), promote innovations for climate-neutral cities (regulatory changes, new business models, and implementing testbeds and living labs), and develop leadership skills for sustainability transitions (mobilizing resources, inspiring new ideas, and developing pilot projects; Farhangi et al., 2023). These desired skills of urban planners as well as obstacles for their implementation are further investigated in interviews and collaborative workshops with Swedish municipalities, while at the same time suggestions and templates are developed for how these can be incorporated into urban and regional planning education programs at Swedish universities. In addition, educational material and workshops are developed to improve the transition-related skills of those already working in urban planning and being in need of continuous learning. With planners trained to foster urban sustainability transitions it will also become more feasible to adapt organizational and governance structures in cities that allow to apply these skills in a more effective way and thereby better align individual and organizational capacities for urban transformation.

CONCLUSIONS

Making cities and human settlements inclusive, safe, resilient, and sustainable as set out in the SDGs to be achieved by 2030 requires fundamental change processes in terms of technologies, social practices, and institutional structures. Governing such processes of transformative change in cities poses new types of challenges and demands on urban governance. In this chapter, we have argued that this requires new individual competences and organizational capacities in municipal administrations, including the capacity to facilitate collaboration with a broad range of urban actors from business and civil society and the cooperation in multi-level governance arrangements between local, regional, national, and transnational levels. Universities and other higher education institutions can play an important role in fostering urban sustainability transitions and in developing new urban capacities for transformative change.

This orientation toward societal challenges and a closer collaboration with practitioners and other non-academic actors poses a formidable challenge for university research as well. New "ways of knowing" are needed as much as new forms of knowledge integration and problem formulation in joint arenas with societal actors. This is reflected in new forms of research organization such as transdisciplinary research or post-normal science.

In this chapter, we have presented some examples of how universities and cities can collaborate in different ways, be it through transdisciplinary research and collaboration on new forms of learning-oriented monitoring and the development of new types of indicators for transformative change toward climate neutrality, be it through new forms of transdisciplinary PhD education in close collaboration with municipal practitioners, or be it by adapting the education of urban and regional planners to the challenges of a transition toward sustainable cities. All these examples can crucially contribute to improve the knowledge base and the capacity to govern urban sustainability transitions.

However, despite their growing number, such examples of transdisciplinary collaboration are still not the norm and the potential contribution of higher education to urban sustainability remains under-exploited. Cultural and organizational changes both at universities and in municipalities as well as in their interaction are needed to make these so far isolated efforts the new normal. Intermediary organizations, such as the program Viable Cities described in this chapter, can play an important role in this cultural change. They can provide stable structures and fora which facilitate joint learning between cities, universities, and other societal actors and ultimately create the capacities needed for urban governance toward sustainability and climate neutrality.

NOTES

1. https://viablecities.se/en/om/

2. https://viablecities.se/en/klimatneutrala-stader-2030/transition-lab/

3. https://liu.se/en/research/just-transitions-research-school

REFERENCES

Berglund-Snodgrass, L., & Mukhtar-Landgren, D. (2020). Conceptualizing testbed planning: Urban planning in the intersection between experimental and public sector logics. *Urban Planning*, 5(1), 11.

Bulkeley, H., & Castán Broto, V. (2013). Government by experiment? Global cities and the governing of climate change. *Transactions of the Institute of British Geographers*, 38(3), 361–375.

Bulkeley, H., Castán Broto, V., Hodson, M., & Marvin, S. (Eds.). (2011). *Cities and low carbon transitions*. Routledge.

Bulkeley, H., Marvin, S., Pagan, Y. V., McCormick, K., Breitfuss-Loidl, M., Mai, L., von Wirth, T., & Frantzeskaki, N. (2019). Urban living laboratories: Conducting the experimental city? *European Urban and Regional Studies*, 26(4), 317–335.

Castán Broto, V., Trencher, G., Iwaszuk, E., & Westman, L. (2019). Transformative capacity and local action for urban sustainability. *Ambio*, 48(5), 449–462.

Dunlop, T., & Völker, T. (2023). The politics of measurement and the case of energy efficiency policy in the European Union. *Energy Research & Social Science*, 96, 102918.

Elmqvist, T., Andersson, E., Frantzeskaki, N., McPhearson, T., Olsson, P., Gaffney, O., Takeuchi, K., & Folke, C. (2019). Sustainability and resilience for transformation in the urban century. *Nature Sustainability*, 2(4), 267–273.

Engels, F., Wentland, A., & Pfotenhauer, S. M. (2019). Testing future societies? Developing a framework for test beds and living labs as instruments of innovation governance. *Research Policy*, 48(9), 103826.

Etzkowitz, H., & Leydesdorff, L. (2000). The dynamics of innovation: From national systems and "Mode 2" to a triple helix of university–industry–government relations. *Research Policy*, 29, 109–123.

Evans, J., Karvonen, A., & Raven, R. (Eds.). (2016). *The experimental city*. Routledge.

Farhangi, M., Magnusson, D., Rohracher, H., Skill, K., & Trygg, K. (2023). Planning education and transformative capacity for climate-neutral cities. *Journal of Planning Education and Research*. Epub ahead of print November 26. doi: 10.1177/0739456X231211572.

Felt, U., Igelsböck, J., Schikowitz, A., & Völker, T. (2016). Transdisciplinary sustainability research in practice: Between imaginaries of collective experimentation and entrenched academic value orders. *Science, Technology & Human Values*, 41(4), 732–161.

Frantzeskaki, N., Castán Broto, V., Coenen, L., & Loorbach, D. (Eds.). (2017). *Urban sustainability transitions*. Routledge.

Geels, F. W. (2005). *Technological transitions and system innovations. A co-evolutionary and socio-technical analysis*. Edward Elgar.

Gibbons, M., Limoges, C., Nowotny, H., Schwartzman, S., Scott, P., & Trow, M. (1994). *The new production of knowledge. The dynamics of science and research in contemporary societies*. Sage.

Haddad, C. R., & Bergek, A. (2023). Towards an integrated framework for evaluating transformative innovation policy. *Research Policy*, 52(2), 104676.

Hestad, D., Tàbara, J. D., & Thornton, T. F. (2021). The role of sustainability-oriented hybrid organisations in the development of transformative capacities: The case of Barcelona. *Cities*, 119, 103365.

Hölscher, K., Frantzeskaki, N., McPhearson, T., & Loorbach, D. (2019). Capacities for urban transformations governance and the case of New York City. *Cities*, 94, 186–199.

Jahn, T., Bergmann, M., & Keil, F. (2012). Transdisciplinarity: Between mainstreaming and marginalization. *Ecological Economics*, 79, 1–10.

Karvonen, A., & van Heur, B. (2014). Urban laboratories: Experiments in reworking cities. *International Journal of Urban and Regional Research*, 38(2), 379–392.

Kivimaa, P., Boon, W., Hyysalo, S., & Klerkx, L. (2019). Towards a typology of intermediaries in sustainability transitions: A systematic review and a research agenda. *Research Policy*, 48(4), 1062–1075.

Klein, J. T. (2014). Discourses of transdisciplinarity: Looking back to the future. *Futures*, *63*(0), 68–74.

Köhler, J., Geels, F. W., Kern, F., Markard, J., Wieczorek, A., Alkemade, F., Avelino, F., Bergek, A., Boons, F., Fünfschilling, L., Hess, D., Holtz, G., Hyysalo, S., Jenkins, K., Kivimaa, P., Martiskainen, M., McMeekin, A., Mühlemeier, M. S., Nykvist, B., ... Wells, P. (2019). An agenda for sustainability transitions research: State of the art and future directions. *Environmental Innovation and Societal Transitions*, *31*, 1–32.

Lyytimäki, J. (2019). Thermostat or thermometer? A Finnish perspective on the overloaded role of sustainability indicators in societal transition. *Sustainable Development*, *27*(5), 817–825.

Mazzucato, M. (2018). Mission-oriented innovation policies: challenges and opportunities. *Industrial and Corporate Change*, *27*(5), 803–815.

McAdam, M., & Debackere, K. (2018). Beyond 'triple helix' toward 'quadruple helix' models in regional innovation systems: Implications for theory and practice. *R&D Management*, *48*(1), 3–6.

Molas-Gallart, J., Boni, A., Giachi, S., & Schot, J. (2021). A formative approach to the evaluation of transformative innovation policies. *Research Evaluation*, *30*(4), 431–442.

Mukhtar-Landgren, D., Kronsell, A., Voytenko Palgan, Y., & von Wirth, T. (2019). Municipalities as enablers in urban experimentation. *Journal of Environmental Policy & Planning*, *21*(6), 718–733.

Nowotny, H., Scott, P., & Gibbons, M. (2001). *Re-thinking Science. Knowledge and the public in an age of uncertainty*. Polity Press.

Peris-Blanes, J., Segura-Calera, S., Arabia, N., & Rib-Pérez, D. (2022). The role of place in shaping urban transformative capacity. The case of València (Spain). *Environmental Innovation and Societal Transitions*, *42*, 124–137.

Ravetz, J. R. (2011). Postnormal Science and the maturing of the structural contradictions of modern European science. *Futures*, *43*(2), 142–148.

Renn, O. (2021). Transdisciplinarity: Synthesis towards a modular approach. *Futures*, *130*, 102744.

Rohracher, H., & Ornetzeder, M. (2019). Sustainable innovation as a challenge for urban governance. In F. Boons & A. McMeekin (Eds.), *Handbook of sustainable innovation* (pp. 268–280). Edward Elgar.

Rohracher, H., & Späth, P. (2014). The interplay of urban energy policy and socio-technical transitions: The eco-cities of Graz and Freiburg in retrospect. *Urban Studies, 51*(7), 1413–1429.

Romero-Lankao, P., Bulkeley, H., Pelling, M., Burch, S., Gordon, D. J., Gupta, J., Johnson, C., Kurian, P., Lecavalier, E., Simon, D., Tozer, L., Ziervogel, G., & Munshi, D. (2018). Urban transformative potential in a changing climate. *Nature Climate Change, 8*(9), 754–756.

Schot, J., & Steinmueller, W. E. (2018). Three frames for innovation policy: R&D, systems of innovation and transformative change. *Research Policy, 47*(9), 1554–1567.

Smith, A., & Raven, R. (2012). What is protective space? Reconsidering niches in transitions to sustainability. *Research Policy, 41*(6), 1025–1036.

Torrens, J., Westman, L., Wolfram, M., Broto, V. C., Barnes, J., Egermann, M., Ehnert, F., Frantzeskaki, N., Fratini, C. F., Håkansson, I., Hölscher, K., Huang, P., Raven, R., Sattlegger, A., Schmidt-Thomé, K., Smeds, E., Vogel, N., Wangel, J., & von Wirth, T. (2021). Advancing urban transitions and transformations research. *Environmental Innovation and Societal Transitions, 41*, 102–105.

Trencher, G., Yarime, M., McCormick, K. B., Doll, C. N. H., & Kraines, S. B. (2014). Beyond the third mission: Exploring the emerging university function of co-creation for sustainability. *Science and Public Policy, 41*(2), 151–179.

Truffer, B., Rohracher, H., Kivimaa, P., Raven, R., Alkemade, F., Carvalho, L., & Feola, G. (2022). A perspective on the future of sustainability transitions research. *Environmental Innovation and Societal Transitions, 42*, 331–339.

Völker, T., Kovacic, Z., & Strand, R. (2020). Indicator development as a site of collective imagination? The case of European Commission policies on the circular economy. *Culture and Organization, 26*(2), 103–120.

Wolfram, M. (2016). Conceptualizing urban transformative capacity: A framework for research and policy. *Cities, 51*, 121–130.

Wolfram, M., Borgström, S., & Farrelly, M. (2019). Urban transformative capacity: From concept to practice. *Ambio*, *48*(5), 437–448.

Yli-Viikari, A. (2009). Confusing messages of sustainability indicators. *Local Environment*, *14*(10), 891–903.

Ziman, J. (1996). "Postacademic science": Constructing knowledge with networks and norms. *Science Studies*, *9*(1), 67–80.

3

WHY CITYSTUDIO, WHY NOW?

Duane Elverum, Alix Linaker and Marga Pacis

CityStudio Vancouver, Canada

ABSTRACT

CityStudio is an adaptable, plug and play model that helps global cities create a permanent partnership with local higher education institutions (HEIs) for collaboration, projects, and mutual benefit. Since launching, CityStudio has seen well over 906 city staff working with 16,861 students on 3,578 projects, contributing well over 300,000 student hours to local civic priorities in three countries. CityStudio assists cities to identify and distribute priority needs to local HEI's universities, providing increased capacity for cities and work-integrated learning opportunities for students on real-world projects in areas such as sustainability, equity, livability, and social justice. While projects directly support local strategic planning goals, they also align with the United Nations Sustainable Development Goals (UNSDGs). The dream of CityStudio is that students take a seat at the table of civic power, joining and helping the city with their needs and challenges for a better planet. But we find ourselves asking, will tomorrow be worse? Worse for democracy, worse for the environment, and worse for equity and choice? In our unique facilitator and translator position between large public institutions, across a growing network, we explore daily how to meet this moment meaningfully.

Keywords: Students; collaboration; civic priorities; partnerships; green cities; Vancouver

INTRODUCTION

CityStudio is an adaptable, plug and play model that helps global cities create a permanent partnership with local HEIs for collaboration, research, projects, and mutual benefit.

Since launching, CityStudio has seen well over 906 city staff working with 16,861 students on 3,578 projects, contributing well over 300,000 student hours to local civic priorities in three countries.

Over the past decade, students at CityStudio have created community gardens, pop-up parks, street furniture, murals, and events. They have also analyzed bike paths, mapped food deserts, proposed land-use policy, and counted intertidal species as well as studied dog waste in parks. CityStudio students have improved settlement services, developed community skill shares, and tested beach-front water quality. They have also presented their work to the city council to show how these projects improve our city and our lives.

CityStudio identifies and distributes priority city needs to local HEI's universities, providing more capacity for cities and work-integrated learning opportunities for students on real-world projects in areas such as sustainability, equity, livability, and social justice. While projects directly support local strategic planning goals, they also align with the UNSDGs, a set of global goals adopted by the United Nations in 2015 to end poverty, protect the planet, and ensure prosperity for all. Specifically, CityStudio projects frequently focus on SDG #11, which aims to make cities and human settlements inclusive, safe, resilient, and sustainable.

The dream of CityStudio is that students take a seat at the table of civic power, joining and helping the city with their needs and challenges for a better planet. But we find ourselves asking, *will tomorrow be worse?* Worse for democracy, worse for the environment, and worse for equity and choice?

In our unique facilitator and translator position between large public institutions, we explore how to meet this moment.

Our focus in the coming decade will be to grow the alignment of CityStudio projects with each of the UNSDG's so that each CityStudio project across a growing network allows students, city staff, and community to see and understand how their work contributes to a comprehensive planetary framework working toward peace and prosperity for people and the planet, now and into the future.

THE ORIGINS OF CITYSTUDIO

In 2010, the City of Vancouver launched an ambitious plan to become the greenest city in the world, seeking big ideas and innovative thinking to lead global sustainability – one of the most ambitious environmental stewardship programs in the world.

At the same time within Simon Fraser University, CityStudio co-founders Dr Janet Moore and Duane Elverum were developing a new pedagogy to engage students and accelerate sustainability with civic action projects. When Vancouver Gregor Mayor Robertson asked citizens to submit the best ideas to meet his Greenest City goals, we submitted our CityStudio project: We proposed that students – with their hope, energy, and enthusiasm – needed to be at the center of the city learning and helping staff solve our most complex problems.

The Deputy City Manager Sadhu Johnston saw multiple benefits, and offered us a studio space under the Cambie bridge. We created a space where, for the first time, city staff, students, faculty, and community members could talk openly about what matters most, develop experimental projects together to test ideas, and plan for ways to make the best project permanent.

CityStudio was established by the City of Vancouver together with six universities as a part of an inter-institutional university–city collaboration, C3, to develop projects and research related to urban sustainability.

It seemed clear that Vancouver needed our schools and students as much as we needed them. In front of 400 people, at the Greenest City Ideas Slam, we proposed the idea of a CityStudio to a panel of 12 community leaders, including the Mayor and city manager. We were invited to set up an experimental class inside city hall with 14 students, working directly with staff on a few projects to support the Greenest City Action Plan. They gave us one year to show how students could contribute; the course showed that students could do far more than we asked them to do in their classes, with an added dimension; city staff were also getting more deeply engaged and asking what else we could design and build.

When assessing a city's readiness to collaborate with post-secondary institutions, we use a Readiness Assessment Checklist that highlights the importance of having top leadership at both the city and post-secondary institutions committed to the collaboration, signaled through a signed memorandum of understanding (MOU).

Since then we have continued our work in Vancouver while growing the network of cities to join us on this journey of civic action, engagement, and innovation through CityStudio's Theory of Change.

HOW WE DEVELOP PROJECTS

Over the past decade, we have developed a project development process which creates high value for city staff, while ensuring significant project-based and work-integrated learning experiences for students.

The foundation of the CityStudio model is based on trust-based relationships, strong buy-in and commitment from leadership, and meaningful projects that are scoped and facilitated by a trained project coordinator to directly serve municipal priorities.

This project work is integrated into classes and course work, providing students the opportunity to contribute energy and action to their cities and towns during school, rather than being asked to save the planet on evenings and weekends. This work requires ongoing collaboration between city staff and faculty, facilitated by a trained and certified, local CityStudio coordinator.

This Project Coordinator plays the key role of matchmaker, finding relevant city projects that align with courses and faculty interest at the school(s). This saves time and resources for the city and school(s) as the need for individual outreach is eliminated.

It is critical that the Project Coordinator establishes trust-based relationships with interested partners prior to projects starting. Without a basis of solid relationships, quality project development, matching, and implementation are not sustainable.

For this reason, the Project Coordinator first seeks connections with City staff and leadership who have expressed openness and excitement around civic innovation and collaboration. It is important to consider if leaders, city staff, and faculty understand experiential service learning and if connections to faculty running project-based courses already exist. The coordinator works with city staff, faculty, and students to develop projects with an annual cycle that consists of five steps:

1. *Convene city staff*: City staff is convened to identify and develop project ideas that further the city's strategic aims. For example, projects to enhance social inclusion in communities, increase neighborhood resilience, decrease stigma around mental health, decrease residents' carbon footprints, and increase voter turnout. This meeting is organized and facilitated by a Project Coordinator.

2. *Match projects with schools*: Project ideas are matched with courses at partner schools, ensuring a strong fit between city needs and faculty expertise.

3. *Design projects together*: As part of their coursework, students work together with city staff (for class credit) to scope and co-create neighborhood-based projects.

4. *Launch projects in public*: Students launch projects in public as experiments, prototypes, pilots, or engagement events in order to test what works.

5. *Share and scale projects*: Across the network, projects are presented at the HUBBUB celebratory showcase inside City Hall where city staff, faculty, citizens, elected officials, and students connect to discuss how these projects can inform next steps, or become permanent solutions for the city.

OUR THEORY OF CHANGE

At CityStudio, learning how to lead and convene their network of multiple stakeholders, who often have differing agendas, has been an iterative process, leading to two key lessons that shaped a systematic approach to collaboration. First, that trust-based relationships are a necessary prelude to collaboration. This important lesson was learned because we were trying, and often struggling, to undertake projects before we fully understood the stakeholders.

We have seen that our mission hinges in large part on the quality of individual relationships. Previously, the initial idea that projects would be the first step in our theory of change (Fig. 3.1), compromised both the longevity and quality of project impacts. Attempts to then build this trust, however, presented the second lesson, that the trust can be an outcome of effective dialogue. With our organization serving as a backbone organization, we aim to build and establish this trust by demonstrating impartial and mutual facilitation and convening. It takes work and expertise to amplify and integrate the agendas of stakeholders.

With this as a key set of practices, the CityStudio in the network works together with each of its collaborators and network members communicating in real time with all other members. Our future work will evaluate how best to understand and facilitate this in order to optimize opportunities to communicate and learn with one another.

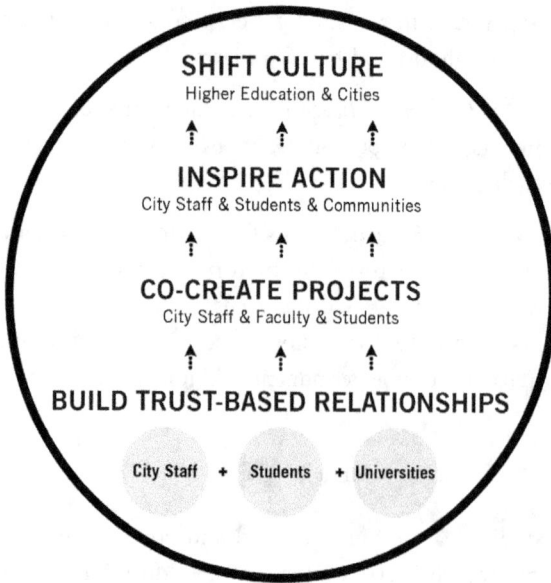

Fig. 3.1. Theory of Change.

Source: Elverum, D., & Moore, J. (2014). Copyright CityStudio, Copyright Janet Moore.

OUR IMPACT

By working together, students, faculty, and city staff across our network have the potential to create a significant collective impact. The results of our six-year impact survey (Fig. 3.2) show that city staff are better able to look for creative engagement opportunities for students to help identify and solve challenges, and to recognize the influential role students can have in affecting systemic change in certain city services and planning areas.

Systemic change demands that our public institutions work together more easily and more often. The CityStudio model demonstrates that successful systems change work is relational. CityStudio is an example of a social innovation contributing to the way cities and post-secondary institutions work together for civic benefit.

THE SOCIO-ECONOMIC CONTEXT

In addition to the impact noted above, the CityStudio model can positively contribute to the current socio-economic challenges facing cities, post-secondary institutions, and students. Specifically, the

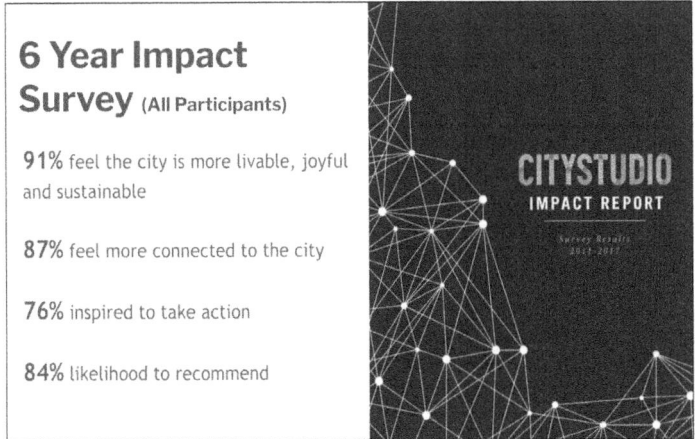

Fig. 3.2. Six-year Impact Survey.
Source: Moore, J., & Elverum, D. (2014). Copyright CityStudio, Copyright Janet Moore.

CityStudio model takes the relationship between the society and the economy into account in three ways:

1. *The city as corporate entity*: In terms of the city as a corporate entity, inviting youth to take a seat at the table of decision-making and action has been shown to have significant mutual benefits: the city and city staff not only gain support on key priorities, but also benefit from insights and energies of the youth demographic. City staff also report greater risk and experimentation tolerance, as well as key insights, into the lived experience that young citizens encounter in their daily lives, as a result of working together on the same problem.

2. *The students as learners and young citizens*: As young citizens contributing to their cities through project work, students illuminate the socio-economic landscape in two fundamental ways: on one hand, their projects provide a work-integrated learning experience that includes skill awareness and building as well as pre-professional relational awareness, both of which help with understanding and mapping their career landscape. Additionally, projects provide a direct path toward civic action and engagement as well as a growing awareness of the crucial role cities play at the intersection of the climate emergency, equity, and democracy.

3. *The post-secondary institutions*: Post-secondary institutions are increasingly asked by students and industry to provide more and more relevant opportunities for students to gain career experiences and skills, as well as general workforce readiness. Graduating into significant debt, and largely without skills to navigate careers in the era of disruptive economies, the climate emergency, equitable society, and healthy democracy, students are energetically seeking more and better opportunities during their education. The CityStudio model provides students with avenues to address these needs while they are in their classes, as an integral part of their education, in preparation for graduation.

PROJECT EXAMPLES

At CityStudio, our projects are at the center of the work and are designed to prepare students for effective, collaborative careers focused on advancing sustainability through local community plans. Through hands-on experiential learning opportunities, CityStudio helps students develop the skills and knowledge they need to be effective change-makers in their communities.

Students have the opportunity to work on real-world projects that address local challenges such as sustainability, livability, and social justice. These projects often relate to the SDGs and provide students with the opportunity to make a positive impact in their communities.

In addition to providing students with practical experience, CityStudio also helps students develop important skills such as collaboration, communication, and problem-solving. By working with city staff, community organizations, and local residents on projects, students learn how to effectively collaborate with diverse stakeholders and navigate complex issues.

Overall, CityStudio's focus on student projects helps to prepare students for careers focused on advancing the SDGs, particularly SDG #11. By providing students with the skills and resources they need to be effective change-makers, CityStudio is helping to cultivate the next generation of urban leaders who are committed to building more sustainable and equitable cities.

Local Community Gardens

At CityStudio, in 2017, students worked with the City of Vancouver and the Vancouver Park Board to develop a plan for a new community garden in an underserved neighborhood. The project involved engaging with local residents to gather feedback and ideas, and resulted in a detailed plan for the garden, which was eventually built and is now being maintained by the community.

Sustainable Transportation

At CityStudio London, in 2019, students partnered with a local housing association to develop a program to encourage sustainable transportation habits among residents. The project involved conducting research on transportation patterns in the community and developing a marketing campaign to promote the use of public transportation, walking, and biking.

Reuse

At CityStudio Bendigo, in 2018, students worked with the City of Greater Bendigo and local schools to develop a program to promote the use of reusable water bottles. The project involved designing and distributing reusable water bottles to students and teachers, as well as developing educational materials about the environmental impacts of single-use plastic water bottles.

Extreme Heat Response

At CityStudio North Vancouver, in 2022, students from Capilano University designed a project to support North Shore Emergency Management to identify knowledge gaps and address challenges associated with their ability to prepare for and respond to the growing frequency and severity of extreme weather events. Of particular focus are those groups which face disproportionate impacts from extreme weather events, including people with existing health issues who may lack coping capacity, and/or those with socio-economic challenges who face higher relative risk exposure due to inadequate housing and limited access to protective infrastructure.

Food Security

CityStudio Abbotsford, in 2021, worked with students at the University of the Fraser Valley to help non-profit organizations to address the issue of food security in the local community. The students created inclusive and people-centered materials to feature the Fraser Valley Food Connections' new Food Program and model, thus contributing to a more equitable, and livable Abbotsford.

Active Transportation

At CityStudio Bendigo, in 2022, students at La Trobe University designed a project called Fitness, Finance, and Fresh Air: The three F's of active transport, focused on active transport in and around Bendigo's Central Business District (CBD), to provide awareness and encourage workers that live in proximity to CBD that walking and cycling to work is an option. The project assisted city staff to help the community increase sustainable and active transport participation in order to meet targets set out in Bendigo's Climate Change and Environment Strategy 2021–2026.

Children's Readiness for School

CityStudio Durham, working with Durham College students on a seven-week placement in 2021, developed research and tools to help teachers and administrators stay informed about children's development and readiness for school, supporting the developmental health of Durham Region children across five domains: (1) physical health and well-being; (2) social competence; (3) emotional maturity; (4) language and cognitive development; and (5) communication skills and general knowledge.

Youth Engagement

In 2022, students from UBC worked within the Sea2City Design Challenge and Climate Change Adaptation Strategy on a project called 100 Postcards from the Future. Sea2City is a design challenge to creatively respond to the social, economic, and environmental challenges of sea-level rise and coastal flooding in Vancouver. 100 UBC Design students in the Design, Culture, and Ecology course (DES 130), taught by Dr Allison Earl, each created a postcard that demonstrated a values-based design for an assigned site at False Creek from the perspective of a stakeholder they chose.

A STORY OF PERSONAL TRANSFORMATION

Margarita Pacis, CityStudio Alumna, Current City of Vancouver Staff

My CityStudio journey has come full circle. I am a CityStudio alumna, and now I have the privilege of collaborating with CityStudio cohorts through my work at the City of Vancouver. After graduating with a Bachelor of Science in Biology, I realized that my passions exist at the intersection of science and engagement. I wanted health well into the years ahead. From our position, we are seeing municipal governments and youth around the world thrust to the front lines of these challenges, which will almost certainly characterize our next decade.

This movement is inevitable, turbocharging the social and systems transformation potential is built into our CityStudio mission. The dream of CityStudio is that students take a seat at the table of civic power, joining and helping the city with their needs and challenges. After more than a decade of this work, I believe we have learned a lot about how to transform technical concepts about sustainability into action at the community level.

During the Master's program, we peeled back layers of Vancouver to learn about local sustainability challenges and opportunities. We became comfortable being uncomfortable by engaging in dialogue that disrupted our frames of reference and transformed our ways of thinking. We learned to trust the process, even if the process was messy. The program was place-based and experiential; we learned in canoes, in tree canopies, and on the seawall. Our projects involved place-making and had real world impacts on the city. As you create place, it shapes you too, and these real-world projects have helped form my path.

I am always incredibly excited to collaborate with CityStudio, and have worked on projects that investigate equity metrics in climate plans, urban greening, and sea level rise. These collaborations always inspire me to think in different ways and seek out ways to improve equity and justice in my work. I strongly believe in creating spaces for youth to participate in civic processes; I have benefited from the connections CityStudio has facilitated between local government and students, and I hope to create similar opportunities for youth.

OUR NEXT DECADE

Now, after a decade of relative stability, many organizations like ours have experienced a significant turning point: imagine Canada's 2021 study which found that close to half of non-profits are struggling with a 40% cut to services and staff this past year, despite a growing need for these services. This marks the beginning of a long and challenging sector reset, as organizations try to find their footing, stabilize services, and secure funding.

The foreseeable future is bringing other challenges: our growing population and our communities and governments will certainly struggle with affordability, equity, inclusion, and climate to take on the much bigger challenges that lay ahead.

It is our hope that this chapter has provided an overview of how we are creating long lasting and productive connections between HEIs and municipalities as we all aim to understand and speed the urban transformation processes around the world. Our accreditations can be seen in Fig. 3.3.

Visit www.citystudio.co to learn more.

Fig. 3.3. Recognition.
Source: Elverum, D., & Moore, J. (2014). Copyright CityStudio, Copyright Janet Moore.

4

PRIORITIZING PRINCIPLES OF JUSTICE AND COLLABORATIVE RESEARCH IN AN AFRICAN HIGHER EDUCATION INSTITUTION IN ORDER TO ADVANCE URBAN SUSTAINABILITY: THE URBAN FUTURES CENTRE (DURBAN UNIVERSITY OF TECHNOLOGY) IN SOUTH AFRICA

Jennifer Houghton[a] and Bakhetsile Mangena[b]

[a]*Department of Town and Regional Planning, Durban University of Technology, South Africa*
[b]*The Independent Institute of Education, South Africa*

ABSTRACT

The African continent is confronted with multiple sustainability concerns that endanger the natural environment and the socio-economic well-being of its people, particularly in rapidly growing cities. Higher education institutions (HEIs) are recognized as crucial agents for enhancing the continent's sustainable development initiatives. The mobilization of African HEIs' resources, researchers, and graduates can assist in striving to meet the priorities for sustainable urban environments laid out in Sustainable Development Goal 11 (SDG11), however, this requires shifts away from traditional academic practices in persistently challenging institutional and urban contexts. In this chapter, the authors focus on the Urban Futures Centre (UFC) at the Durban University of Technology (DUT) in South Africa in order to highlight the potential utility of alternative forms of scholarship and theory building in African HEIs. Foundational to the Centre's work is a concern for the quality of life of the real people who live in cities, and their futures. To this end, a small multidisciplinary staff and post-graduate students undertake projects addressing, for example, harm reduction for homeless drug users; place-making and belonging in marginalized communities; and localized responses to severe urban flooding. These projects typically utilize collaborative, interdisciplinary, and applied approaches. The authors draw on a range of projects undertaken by the Centre in the last five years, encompassing numerous urban realities, varying goals, methodologies, and stakeholder engagement. These projects show how scholarship underpinned by principles of social and environmental justice and the prioritization of shared knowledge production is central to advancing the responsiveness of HEIs to the goals of SDG11 in African cities and beyond.

Keywords: Social inclusion; alternative scholarship; higher education; university organizational challenges; African cities; urban sustainability

INTRODUCTION

The African continent faces sustainability challenges, threatening the environment and socio-economic well-being, especially in rapidly growing cities. Higher education reform is crucial for achieving the SDGs, particularly SDG11, which aims to make cities and human settlements more inclusive, safe, resilient, and sustainable (Ochoa-Hernández & Munguía, 2019). HEIs play a crucial role in promoting sustainable development in Africa. In this chapter, we focus on the UFC at the DUT in South Africa in order to highlight the potential utility of alternative forms of scholarship and theory building in African HEIs. Foundational to the Centre's work is a concern for the quality of life of the real people who live in cities, and their futures. They employ a small team of multidisciplinary staff and post-graduate students to undertake projects addressing issues such as the value of marine resources, harm reduction for homeless drug users, place-making in marginalized communities, and localized responses to urban flooding. We draw on a range of projects undertaken by the Centre in the last five years, encompassing numerous urban realities, varying goals and methodologies, and different frameworks of funding and stakeholder engagement. The experiences and outcomes of these projects demonstrate how scholarship underpinned by principles of social and environmental justice and the prioritization of shared knowledge production is central to advancing the responsiveness of HEIs to the goals of SDG11 in African cities and beyond.

HIGHER EDUCATION AND THE IMPLEMENTATION OF SDG11

The 2030 Agenda for Sustainable Development advocates for a fundamental transition resulting in a revolution in how people handle nature, create and consume, distribute values, and ensure an inclusive, fair, and equitable society (Richardson, 2014; United Nations, 2015). Education is a driving force behind the establishment of sustainability since it is one of the primary communication mediums of these approaches and the foundation for the "sustainability mindset" which requires that systemic thinking replaces traditional disciplinary silos of knowledge and practice (Kassel et al., 2018; UNESCO, 2014, 2019). Richardson (2014) argues that it is the social obligation of universities and the academic communities they create to encourage and defend sustainability transitions, as well as to reflect on and demonstrate their resultant challenges and repercussions. To this end, the resources of HEIs, their academic practices, and their production of knowledge and skills are crucial in progressing these shifts (Godfrey & Zhou, 2017; Hallinger & Chatpinyakoop, 2019; Ochoa-Hernández & Munguía, 2019).

HEIs work to promote sustainable development by incorporating the SDGs' concepts and objectives into their teaching, research, and campus operations (Adams et al., 2018; UNESCO, 2019). Higher education reform toward the SDGs is a significant and multidimensional project. HEIs are critical to meeting SDG11, which focuses on sustainable cities and communities because they can provide the next generation with the skills, knowledge, and understanding needed to address sustainability challenges and opportunities, as well as conduct research that advances the sustainable development agenda (Adams et al., 2018; Cohen & Dalberto, 2020). Across the world, HEIs have been involved in modifying their curricula to include ideas of sustainable development and urban sustainability over many decades. It is increasingly commonplace for universities to be undertaking teaching and research focused on sustainable urban development, sustainable architecture and design, climate change mitigation and adaptation, urban governance, social inclusion, environmental science, renewable energy, and other SDG11-related areas (Boarin et al., 2020; Jucker & Mather, 2017; Sonetti et al., 2019).

In terms of research, knowledge production, and innovation, there has been a movement away from the separateness of the "ivory tower" to HEIs contributing to change through multidisciplinary research collaborations and initiatives that solve urban issues and assist SDG11 target execution (Adams et al., 2018). They collaborate with local governments, non-governmental organizations, and community organizations to address pressing urban issues as the need arises as well as through programs aimed at producing long-term solutions (Boarin et al., 2020; Brown, 2019). This can include community- and place-based research, service-learning programs, and partnership-based collaborations and co-production to improve the quality of life in metropolitan regions (Adams et al., 2018). Universities (HEIs) are frequently slow pace to adapt to society's requirements, and there is widespread agreement that they must evolve into sustainable organizations (Ezquerra-Lázaro et al., 2021). This necessitates moving beyond campus greening and infusing ideals of sustainable development into teaching, research, operations, and community engagement (Ezquerra-Lázaro et al., 2021). HEIs have been divided into highly specialized and unconnected divisions since the 19th century, making it difficult to fund complicated tasks, educate workers, and communicate information (Ezquerra-Lázaro et al., 2021). As a result, universities must evolve to become sustainable organizations that guide society's long-term growth.

Furthermore, universities themselves may serve as models for sustainable urban development and inspire students and the wider community by developing sustainable campuses (Brown, 2019). Implementing energy-efficient infrastructure, supporting waste reduction and recycling programs, encouraging sustainable mobility alternatives, and incorporating green areas into campus design are all examples of sustainability shifts taking place on campuses which emphasize the application of learning and best practice and the necessary shifts in understanding and discourse if global transitions are to take place (Brown, 2019).

Like many HEIs across the world, African institutions endeavor to support sustainability and are highly engaged in teaching students to grasp global concerns and to be active players and role models in implementing sustainability principles. Research activities also play a significant role in how these institutions work toward improving sustainability, particularly in contexts of under-development, rapid urban growth, and limited resources. In the following section, we will demonstrate how one university research center in an African institution of higher education prioritizes principles of social and environmental justice, as well as shared knowledge generation, in order to facilitate the real and deep changes which are needed to accomplish SDG11 priorities and improve life in cities.

THE UFC, DUT

The UFC is a small research center based in the Faculty of Engineering and Built Environment at the DUT in Durban, South Africa. According to the Urban Futures Centre's (UFC, 2023) webpage, the UFC "is an interdisciplinary laboratory that not only builds theory but also tests out ideas and interventions in ways that are not prescribed and determined by dominant stakeholders, be they government officials, academics or large social movements." The guiding principles of the Centre are:

- Using an imaginary lens.
- Doing engaged research.
- Focusing on social and environmental justice.
- Knowledge building for societal good.
- Designing with conscience.
- Aiming for resilience and inclusivity.
- Improving the quality of everyday life in cities.
- Recognizing multiagent systems of governance.
- Challenging dominant paradigms of policy and theorizing (UFC, 2023).

Under the umbrella of these guiding principles, the Centre has a number of core research themes that direct the focus of its work. These are:

- Urban safety and risk management.
- Urban mobility and flows.
- Urban creativity, esthetics, and cultural dynamism.
- The governance of transition and the transition of governance.
- Digital and invisible cities (UFC, 2023).

These principles and core research themes align well with the priorities of the 2030 United Nations Sustainable Development Goals,[1] and, in particular, that of SDG11 to "make cities and human settlements inclusive, safe, resilient, and sustainable." From this foundation, the UFC utilizes university-based capacity and resources to work toward designing sustainable urban solutions to everyday problems. The research undertaken by the Centre is solutions driven, with collaborative efforts, and concern for equality, inclusion, and sustainable urban development at the heart of projects. In addition to being well aligned to the priority areas of SDG11, the methodologies adopted by the Centre work to stimulate participation, creativity, and invention, all of which are required to support and embody the kind of multidisciplinary, systemic transitions and transformations required for sustainable development.

PROJECTS UNDERTAKEN THROUGH THE UFC

As a multidisciplinary center, the project portfolio of the UFC is diverse and has emerged and evolved in response to city-related sustainability needs while operating within the framework of the abovementioned principles, goals, and conceptual lens (Pereverza, 2022). The range of projects that will be drawn upon in discussions within this chapter has been initiated during the last five years, with a number still ongoing. These are not the full scope of projects being undertaken in the UFC but have been selected for discussion as they represent the kinds of engaged scholarship activities which are the main focus of the Centre and provide a collective contribution to the systemic changes required to accomplish SDG11 (Pereverza, 2022). Table 4.1 provides a summary of projects discussed in this chapter.

PRIORITIZING PRINCIPLES OF SOCIAL AND ENVIRONMENTAL JUSTICE

Making the city more sustainable as per SDG11 requires research which adheres to, upholds, and advances the principles of social and environmental justice which lie at the heart of sustainability. Collectively, the projects highlighted here prioritize both social and environmental justice, although the emphasis differs from project to project. The Bellhaven Harm Reduction Centre, Narratives of Home and Neighbourhood, and Welbedacht East projects are explicitly centered on social justice, inclusion, and equity. The other projects address what could be considered primarily "green" environmental issues but take an approach in which socio-environmental relationships are prioritized.

Inclusion and belonging, often fostered through urban place-making, are important features of social justice in cities (Marks et al., 2022; Marks & Moodley, 2021) in that they address the needs of current generations and typically prioritize those who

Table 4.1 Summary of Urban Future Centre Projects Discussed in this Chapter.

Project	Time Frame	Funder	Main Focus Areas	Methodology	Social and Environmental Justice	Knowledge Production
Narratives of Home and Neighbourhood	2017–2019	South African National Research Foundation (Blue Skies Grant)	Place-making and belonging in marginalized communities	Partnership-based project, Participatory action research, Photo voice, Interviews, Focus groups, Public engagement	Sharing of narratives within and between communities	Co-production of knowledge, Formal knowledge sharing – seminars, conference presentations, innovation in housing design publications, including a book

Lalela Ulwandle	2019–ongoing	One Ocean Hub – United Kingdom Research and Innovation Through Global Challenges Fund	Marine resources Cultural value of the ocean and marine resources Global environmental change Awareness raising	Partnership-based project Qualitative Oral histories Interviews Field observations Scripting of primary data into a theatrical piece for dramatic performance with a participatory process of discussion with audiences	Participatory research methodology Shared narratives Shifting narratives and discourses related to the ocean Raising awareness of alternative, typically marginalized, perspectives	Co-production of knowledge across partners Sharing indigenous knowledge COP and United Nations Headquarters visits and theatrical production of Lalela Ulwandle

(Continued)

Table 4.1 Summary of Urban Future Centre Projects Discussed in this Chapter.

Project	Time Frame	Funder	Main Focus Areas	Methodology	Social and Environmental Justice	Knowledge Production
Welbedacht East Place-making	2022–ongoing	Unfunded, voluntary engagement, supported by project partners, including the Welbedacht Civic Association and eThekwini Municipality	Place-making and belonging in marginalized communities Long-term outcomes of state resettlement programs Community building Post-apartheid transitions	Partnership-based project Interviews Community engagement Bridging between city representatives and community representatives Public events and engagement	Community-driven exhibition – Welbedacht is a Beautiful Place Welbedacht Civic Association (UFC, 2023) Participatory planning for "pocket parks" Participatory research methodology	A case study of social cohesion Community events and celebration Place-making practices Community resilience "The WCA has even been working closely with the municipality's War Room for that ward, and as a result of the UFC intervention, the Area Based Management Team now has ongoing engagements with the Civic Association. A priority project has been the establishment" (UFC, 2023, p. 8)

Bellhaven Harm Reduction Centre	2020–ongoing	Advanced Access and Delivery; South African Network of People Who Use Drugs; Open Society Foundations; Love Alliance	Harm reduction Drug use Homelessness Community building Place-making Frugal institutions	Partnership-based project Action research Participatory Embedded research	Engagements with the state to build a platform for policy and practice change Shifts in mindset Shifts in practice Opioid substitution therapy program Emergence of new ongoing projects co-funded by the state Participatory research methodology	Harm reduction Innovations in approach, cutting edge and innovative in the SA context – never done before here

(Continued)

Table 4.1 Summary of Urban Future Centre Projects Discussed in this Chapter.

Project	Time Frame	Funder	Main Focus Areas	Methodology	Social and Environmental Justice	Knowledge Production
Localizing Global Environmental Change: Nexus of Waste, Water, and Society	2019–2023	South African National Research Foundation	Global environmental change Urban governance Localized responses to severe urban flooding Catchment management Solid waste and urban water services Discourses of pollution-related beach closures	Partnership-based project Mixed methods Action research Questionnaire survey Interviews Participation in catchment management forums and policy development processes Discourse analysis	Participation in catchment management forums and policy development processes	Governance platforms Academic and HEIs positionality in relation to sustainability processes

Waste Management, Urban Informality, and Climate Change	2021–2023	Urban Movement Innovation Fund	Zero-waste solutions Pollution reduction Informality Informal markets Green technology and business	Partnership-based project Action research Waste surveying Stakeholder engagement Partnership building and facilitation	Responsiveness to waste stream limitations and challenges Practical application of zero waste and closed loop concepts Food and organic waste diverted from the waste stream Composting Partnerships formation	Upscaling of program to consider business viability and long-term sustainability Community engagement activities in 2022 "enable an exchange of ideas between diverse groupings: waste-pickers, government officials, activists, academics and the wider public, but they have also helped forge greater understanding and solidarity" (UFC, 2023, p. 11)

Sources: Urban Futures Centre (UFC, 2017, 2020, 2021, 2022, 2023).

are most marginalized and vulnerable. One example of this is the UFC program focused on street level drug use and homelessness. In this project, long-term participatory action research, advocacy, and policy-related engagements with the state before and during the COVID-19 pandemic led to a shift in governance and urban public health discourses of street level drug use and homelessness from one of criminality to one of harm reduction (Marks & Moodley, 2021). This has ultimately led to the partnership-driven establishment of the Bellhaven Harm Reduction Centre (the first in Africa). Bellhaven is a community center housed in a public building on the edge of Durban's CBD which has been made available by the City for the purposes of harm reduction of street level drug users. Bellhaven includes a safe-use space, healthcare support, an award-winning methadone clinic with extremely low barriers to entry, computer equipment, leisure spaces, and multiple other social services (Marks & Moodley, 2021; Urban Futures Centre (UFC), 2020, 2021).

In the Narratives of Home and Neighbourhood project, there was a comparison across various poor and middle-class neighborhoods in Durban in order to build a deeper understanding of the meanings of home held by city residents. The neighborhoods included in the study varied in socio-economic and demographic character including a women-only residential hostel, two informal settlements involved in in situ upgrading processes, a number of post-apartheid human settlements, and a middle-class residential neighborhood. The location of these communities was spread across the urban landscape. The diverse choice of neighborhoods ensured the inclusion of different kinds of urban residents in the project and was intended to give a voice to those who often were side-lined or quieted in policy and urban development discourses, even in cases where decision-making would likely directly affect communities (Moodley & Erwin, 2021; Urban Futures Centre (UFC), 2020).

In the case of the Welbedacht project, UFC researchers responded to a need to (re)build social cohesion and overcome racial tensions in Durban which had intensified during a week of city-wide civil unrest and looting in Durban in July 2021 which had broken down trust across the city (UFC, 2023). Welbedacht East, a poor, often overlooked community asserted their wish to focus on their neighborhood as a beautiful place, as a community with strong social ties and social capital, which worked hard to be inclusive of everyone in the neighborhood. The project, allowed for research on place-making and social inclusivity in which individual stories were given voice through interviews, public engagement, a community-focused celebration of the culture and people of Welbedacht and the initiation of dialogue with the local government to develop pocket parks as accessible, inclusive and healthy open spaces within the neighborhood (UFC, 2023). The formulation of the project from the ground up, the inclusion of "ordinary" urban spaces and communities, and the building of partnerships through the research process speak to the nature of research that builds inclusivity and strengthens social bonds, as well as facilitating the highlighting and pride of a community which was poor in many ways but wealthy in terms of social connection (UFC, 2021). As noted in an annual report (Urban Futures Centre (UFC), 2022, p. 8),

> *for the community participants, an important outcome has been the recognition of the value of celebrating their community and changing the ongoing narrative of Welbedacht as an impoverished place where residents live without hope. It was the first time that they were afforded the opportunity to tell the untold stories of community vibrancy and solidarity and not just racial tolerance but real unity and cohesion.*

Other UFC-based research addresses what could be considered primarily "green" environmental issues but take an approach in which socio-environmental relationships are prioritized (UFC, 2020, 2021, 2022). Where the environmental focus is (perhaps) more central, projects purposefully engage with cultural relationships to the natural environment, governance approaches in addressing environmental sustainability, and the prioritization of the relationship between equality and improved quality of the biophysical and living environments of cities.

One example of this focus is Lalela Lwandle, an ongoing climate change-focused project researching cultural understandings of the oceans as a spiritual and physical source of power and life and using these understandings as a foundation for socio-environmental activism. The qualitative methodology and the representation of data through story-telling, dramatic performance, and art highlight the importance of experimental and alternative methodologies (UFC, 2022). These methodologies can maintain the scholarly integrity of research as well as improve the accessibility of research to various audiences, including communities, governments, and multinational organizations; thus prompting new ways of thinking and practice (UFC, 2022).

Ultimately, undertaking research which prioritizes environmental and social justice through the UFC, involves much more than the selection of project focus areas that fit the sustainability mould. The research questions, processes, and outcomes must recognize numerous urban realities and the need to be responsive to particular needs while holding on to the bigger picture of urban sustainability. The ability to reframe (Pereverza, 2022) and reorient actions for sustainability in contexts where practices or discourses are stuck or where resources allow for only so much action is a significant component of research. Here, the UFC researchers are not neutral participants but are actors for change that are perhaps empowered through being set somewhat apart from, but engaging with, the mandates of state actors and the pressing need of those acting from positions of vulnerability and marginalization (Marks, 2020; Marks & Moodley, 2021).

REFLECTIONS ON HEIS IN AFRICA AND THE ADDRESSING OF SDG11

It is reasonable to assert that urban sustainability outcomes in the urban places highlighted above may have been possible even without the role of academics, researchers, and "the university" being involved. Therefore, it is worthwhile considering, the specific ways in which it makes (or should make) a difference to the achieving of SDG11 that these projects take place in and through an urban research center within a university in an African country.

First, and true globally, knowledge production and sharing is a duty of HEIs and in many ways, it is the privilege of academics to integrate knowledge generated within and across projects, to work in applied ways, and to be engaged scholars. The projects discussed here provide a glimpse of the wider benefits of researchers "getting out of the ivory tower" and recognizing that the traditional ways of sharing knowledge and especially those entrenched within the neoliberal global academy will not be sufficient to foster the kinds of knowledge growth, changed understanding, and altered practices that will make cities such as Durban more inclusive and more environmentally sustainable. In the case of research at the UFC, methods of knowledge production are understood to be closely tied to the social and environmental goals and outcomes of projects (UFC, 2023). Inclusiveness is key for sustainable cities and therefore key to methods adopted within research (UFC, 2023). Projects therefore work as bridges between urban actors, many stakeholder groupings, funders, audiences, students, and post-graduate researchers, resulting in shared knowledge production and greater opportunity for sustainability transitions.

The further responsibilities of the HEIs when undertaking these projects are to take the learning and share it, elevate it to broader theorizations, and transfer emergent knowledge into teaching so that it can influence future practice and practitioners. Furthermore, it is necessary to be the conduit for experimental practice that is needed to facilitate transitions toward sustainability in cities and globally. This requires both HEIs and research academics to be "invested" in networked projects of shared, cooperative knowledge building, particularly in urban contexts, where resources are few and capacity is generally limited.

In an African city, where development needs are central and pressing, where the state and the city have few resources, the need for "extra pairs of hands" and people who can think critically, puts academics in close range to the real problems, the communities, places, and a myriad of actors. This creates an ever-present opportunity for HEIs to work much more "on the ground," to get out of, or even dismantle, ivory towers and have the opportunity to integrate research and change; learning and practice; and innovation and responsiveness.

Finally, in doing work which prioritizes social and environmental justice and the shared production of knowledge, one of the things to take cognizance of is the numerous urban realities to be found within and across cities. Ultimately, place matters, and as with the UFC at the DUT, any HEI making real efforts to address SDG11, will need to take places and their contexts into consideration, allowing for flexibility in how work toward achieving the broader goals of SDG11 might play themselves out in a particular context and to "intervene" with sensitivity and, dare one say it, humility, in cooperative processes of learning and change.

NOTE

1. Current and past projects of the UFC have prioritized national research and development goals as well as the United Nations Sustainable Development Goals, including SDG 3 (good health and well-being), 5 (gender equality), 8 (decent work and economic growth), 10 (reduce inequalities), 11 (sustainable cities and communities), 12 (responsible production and consumption), 13 (climate change), 14 (life under water), and 17 (partnership for the goals) (UFC, 2023). In reflecting on UFC projects and processes in this chapter, we will mainly focus on the contributions to SDG11; however, it is to be noted that all SDGs are inherently linked to each other such that working toward a specific goal does not limit the possibilities for positive contributions to any of the other goals. It is also envisaged that the collective gains through the portfolio of UFC projects will be greater than the sum of gains made through individual projects in that they offer entry points to systemic challenges and longer-term shifts (Pereverza, 2022).

REFERENCES

Adams, R., Martin, S., & Boom, K. (2018). University culture and sustainability: Designing and implementing an enabling framework. *Journal of Cleaner Production*, 171, 434–445.

Boarin, P., Martinez-Molina, A., & Juan-Ferruses, I. (2020). Understanding students' perception of sustainability in architecture education: A comparison among universities in three different continents. *Journal of Cleaner Production, 248*, 119237.

Cohen, M. J., & Dalberto, A. R. (2020). The role of higher education institutions in advancing sustainable urban development: A review of the literature. *Journal of Cleaner Production, 251*, 119713.

Ezquerra-Lázaro, I., Gómez-Pérez, A., Mataix, C., Soberón, M., Moreno-Serna, J., & Sánchez-Chaparro, T. (2021). A dialogical approach to readiness for change towards sustainability in higher education institutions: The case of the SDGs seminars at the Universidad Politécnica de Madrid. *Sustainability, 13*, 9168. https://doi.org/10.3390/su13169168

Godfrey, A., & Zhou, P. (2017). Mainstreaming the sustainable development goals into higher education institutions: Challenges and opportunities. *International Journal of Sustainability in Higher Education, 18*(5), 798–818.

Hallinger, P., & Chatpinyakoop, C. (2019). A bibliometric review of research on higher education for sustainable development, 1998–2018. *Sustainability, 11*, 2401.

Jucker, R., & Mathar, R. (2017). *Fostering sustainability at universities: A student-centred toolkit*. Palgrave Macmillan.

Kassel, K., Rimanoczy, I., & Mitchell, S. F. (2018). A sustainable mindset model for management education. In K. Kassel & I. Rimanoczy (Eds.), *Developing a sustainability mindset in management education* (pp. 1–35). Routledge.

Marks, M. (2020). Strangers within: Carving out a role for engaged scholarship in the university space. In K. Henne & R. Shah (Eds.), *Routledge handbook of public criminologies* (pp. 129–137). Routledge.

Marks, M. M., & Moodley, S. (2021). Reaching high: Translating emergent practices of street-level drug users to institute harm reduction in Durban – Implications for urban governance. *Urban Forum, 33*, 485–504.

Marks, M., Moodley, S., & Houghton, J. (2022). *Governing the city through harm reduction: How the Covid-19 crisis created new governance mentalities and technologies in eThekwini* [Working Paper Series]. Paper One contribution to South African Cities Network Cities in Crisis, Cape Town.

Moodley, S. & Erwin, K. (2021). Narratives of Home and Neighbourhood: Rethinking risk in informal and state-delivered settlements in Durban. In R. Beier, A. Spire, & M. Bridonneau (Eds.), *Urban resettlements in the global south: Lived experiences of housing and infrastructure between displacement and relocation* (1st ed., pp. 87–106). Routledge. https://doi.org/10.4324/9781003124559

Ochoa-Hernández, R., & Munguía, N. (2019). A framework for assessing the contribution of higher education institutions to sustainable urban development. *Sustainability, 11*(5), 1463.

Pereverza, K. (2022, June 16). *(Re)framing of challenges in portfolio-based approaches for system transformations*. Medium. https://medium.com/@undp.innovation/re-framing-of-challenges-in-portfolio-based-approaches-for-system-transformations-55cf30f5725c

Richardson, L. (2014). Engaging the public in policy research: Are community researchers the answer? *Politics and Governance, 2*(1), 32–44.

Sonetti, G., Brown, M., & Naboni, E. (2019). About the triggering of UN sustainable development goals and regenerative sustainability in higher education. *Sustainability, 11*, 254.

United Nations. (2015). *Transforming our world: The 2030 agenda for sustainable development*. https://sdgs.un.org/goals/goal11

United Nations Educational, Scientific and Cultural Organization (UNESCO). (2019). *Higher education and the sustainable development goals: The role of universities and research institutions*. http://unesdoc.unesco.org/images/0026/002610/261052E.pdf

United Nations Educational, Scientific and Cultural Organization (UNESCO). (2014). *Roadmap for implementing the global action programme on education for sustainable development*. https://unesdoc.unesco.org/ark:/48223/pf0000227211

Urban Futures Centre (UFC). (2017). *Annual report 2016/2017*. Durban University of Technology. Retrieved May 20, 2023, from https://www.dut.ac.za/wp-content/uploads/2021/01/FINAL_UFC_annual-report_1617_LR.pdf

Urban Futures Centre (UFC). (2020). *Annual report 2019/2020*. Durban University of Technology. Retrieved May 20, 2023, from https://www.dut.ac.za/wp-content/uploads/2021/01/UFC-REPORT-1920.pdf

Urban Futures Centre (UFC). (2021). *Annual report 2021*. Durban University of Technology. Retrieved May 20, 2023, from https://www.dut.ac.za/wp-content/uploads/2022/09/2021-UFC-Annual-Report.pdf

Urban Futures Centre (UFC). (2022). *Bellhaven Harm Reduction Centre annual report 2020–2021*. Retrieved July 15, 2023, from 2020-2021-Bellhaven-Harm-Reduction-Centre-Annual-Report.pdf (dut.ac.za).

Urban Futures Centre (UFC). (2023). *Annual report 2022*. Durban University of Technology. Retrieved May 20, 2023, from https://www.dut.ac.za/wp-content/uploads/2023/06/UFC-Annual-Report-2022-Final.pdf

5

UNIVERSIDAD DE LOS ANDES AND ITS CONTRIBUTION TO BOGOTA IN THE ACHIEVEMENT OF THE 2030 AGENDA

Juan Camilo Cardenas, Manuela Navarrete, Carla Panyella and Mónica Pinilla-Roncancio

Universidad de los Andes, Colombia

ABSTRACT

Universities can play an important role in decarbonizing cities and tackling inequalities in urban settings. Both challenges are particularly critical in Latin America and the Caribbean where demographic transition toward urban areas and the persistent inequalities have increased the ecological footprint of human activities and the economy in general. In this chapter, we will discuss how universities can contribute in a multifaceted manner to the achievement of SDG11, its specific targets, and explore the synergies between SDG11 and other important Sustainable Development Goals (SDGs) in the Latin American and the Caribbean Region. The chapter presents the experience of the Center of the Sustainable Development Goals for Latin America and the Caribbean (CODS) in monitoring the progress in the achievement of the SDGs in the region. In addition, the trajectory of the Universidad de los Andes in Colombia is used to illustrate the challenges and the possibilities for a higher education institution in contributing to moving toward a more sustainable urban setting. These strategies include not only education and research, but also how it has intervened in the immediate neighborhood of the campus, the close ties with the city administration over decades, and close interactions with the private sector at the local and national levels.

Keywords: Sustainable Development Goals; higher education institution; sustainable development; Colombia; urban transformation; sustainable campus

INTRODUCTION

Universities are crucial to decarbonizing and achieving sustainability in cities in both the global north and south. However, universities can also be a source of negative social and environmental impacts on the immediate surroundings of their campuses (Benneworth et al., 2010). The positive contribution usually happens through education and research, and through the establishment of strategic partnerships with actors in the private, social, and public sectors, at local, national, or international levels, and during the implementation of projects whose main objective is to impact positively the society and the physical and social environment of their campuses (Valero & Van Reenen, 2018), while at the same time, avoiding adverse effects on the campus physical and social ecosystems.

The purpose of this chapter is to illustrate, how Universidad de los Andes (Uniandes) in Bogota, Colombia, immersed physically and socially within the city, has built a productive relationship between its academic goals and the community goals. Uniandes is committed to contributing to a sustainable future for its host city, taking into consideration the three spheres of sustainable development, and paying special attention to the challenges that face the city.

Uniandes is in Bogota (the capital of Colombia) and has supported the city's priorities with relevant and pertinent proposals from social, environmental, and economic perspectives in which members of the communities around the campus are involved. Being a young university reaching its 75th anniversary in 2023, Uniandes has actively promoted the creation of spaces and groups where sustainability concerns are the focus. Notably, this includes the creation of the Sustainable Development Goals Center for Latin America and the Caribbean (SDG Center), representing Uniande's commitment in the achievement of the SDGs and leading the progress toward a sustainable future for the city.

Many of the university's sustainability efforts are documented in the annual sustainability report and in the sustainability plan that is published every five years (Universidad de los Andes, 2022c). These documents are of vital importance for the university community as they provide insight into the ongoing actions being undertaken by the university. The report and the strategy facilitate a collaborative process of evaluation and collective development concerning the initiatives that are already underway, as well as the challenges that remain to be addressed, such as mobility, emissions, energy consumption, waste management, among others (Universidad de los Andes, 2021a). The university participates in two distinct rankings that have shed light on its achievements and future challenges. Firstly, there is the UI Green Metric, in which the university has been involved for 13 years, and in 2022, it ranked 11th nationally and 93rd internationally (UI Green Metric, 2022), and, additionally, since 2022, the university has also taken part in the Times Higher Education Impact Ranking, where it also secured the 11th national position (Times Higher Education, 2022). Throughout this journey toward more sustainable practices, the university has strived for transparency and criticality in effecting the transition both from within the campus and extending its influence outward to the city.

UNIVERSIDAD DE LOS ANDES, ITS ROLE AND MOST IMPORTANT CONTRIBUTIONS TO SUSTAINABILITY

Taking as a reference, the guide published by the Sustainable Development Solutions Network (SDSN) on how to accelerate

SDG education in universities, it is clear that the higher education institutions exert influence to achieve the 2030 Agenda and the SDG. According to this guide, higher education institutions can contribute in four major areas, which are: (i) through education and learning, training students with interdisciplinary knowledge who can work on global challenges in the future, as well as promoting affordable and inclusive education; (ii) with research that provides scientific, innovative knowledge with technological solutions that contribute to achieving the goals of the SDGs through interdisciplinary and transdisciplinary approaches, (iii) through institutional governance processes based on the principles of the global Agenda and applying this principle in different instances of the institution, such as employment, finance, etc., as well as (iv) strengthening social leadership from universities, committing different sectors of society to work toward the 2030 Agenda (Sustainable Development Solutions Network, 2020). All these areas, also stress the unifying power of higher education institutions that, thanks to their impartiality and legitimacy within all sectors, can support the articulation with other actors to support the implementation of the 2030 Agenda both locally, nationally, and globally.

Uniandes has been committed to the achievement of the SDGs and the 2030 Agenda since Uniandes looks for academic excellence and provides its students with critical and ethical training to strengthen their awareness of their social and civic responsibilities, as well as their commitment to the environment (Universidad de los Andes, n.d.-c). Uniandes has focused on strengthening alliances with higher education institutions of excellence through regional cooperation mechanisms to encourage research, training, and the exchange of knowledge and experiences around sustainable development (Universidad de los Andes, n.d.-c). Likewise, the University has worked to disseminate the SDGs, not only within its community but also influencing debates and public awareness around the challenges humanity face nowadays. A great example of these spaces to create dialogue about sustainable development is la Catedra Nuestro Futuro organized by the SDG Center for Latina America and the Caribbean.

The creation of the SDG Center at the University supported processes that were already being implemented by the institution to align its strategic objectives with the 2030 Agenda, and to strengthen and catalyze the activities implemented by Uniandes in terms of sustainable development. A driving element for the creation of the Center at Uniandes was that addressing sustainability in an interdisciplinary and transversal way, is an institutional commitment of the University. Taking this into consideration the SDG Center works together with the University to assess the organization's comprehensive contribution to the SDGs, as well as to find opportunities to improve its implementation across different areas of the university. Some examples of this work conducted by the university to map and understand its contribution to the Agenda 2030, is the development of annual reports on how the campus is improving on sustainability issues, as well as, improving their processes and data collection to enhance the organization's contribution toward the Agenda participating in different rankings such as Times Higher Education or the QS Universities Rankings. The final goal is for the SDGs to become a guiding principle for the activities that are implemented by the University, thus permeating not only the education and research programs but all the government structures and relevant spaces of the institution. This goal can be seen clearly reflected in the University's Comprehensive Development Program where it says that "Any strategic planning attempt should start from the Sustainable Development Goals (SDGs) that, together, raise the need to reconcile social development, material progress and environmental sustainability. This task is not only urgent, but also practically a matter of survival" (Universidad de los Andes, 2021b).

One of the central challenges encountered in the establishment of the Center has been the synchronization of initiatives with the diverse academic units within the organization, as well as fostering cross-disciplinary collaboration among professors. An additional significant endeavor has been the cultivation of robust strategic partnerships with regional universities to collectively develop a shared sustainability agenda.

UNIANDES WORK INTERACTING AND LIVING WITHIN A NEIGHBORHOOD AND IN A LARGE CITY

The Fenicia Program

Uniandes, responding to the imperativeness of the urban transformation of the city center of Bogota, decided to take an active role in its urban renewal plans, considering that the central campus is located in this area of the city. With regard to sustainability, the University acknowledges the vital significance of the theory of just urban transitions, as articulated by scholars like Hughes and Hoffmann (2020), who underscore the pivotal and catalytic role played by cities. According to these authors, cities should be envisioned as spaces where the allocation of environmental risks and benefits is equitable and does not unduly burden marginalized communities. They emphasize the need for transparent, participatory, and democratic decision-making processes and advocate for policies that aim to rectify structural inequalities and address past injustices. Triángulo de Fenicia Partial Urban Renovation Plan is an ambitious program that takes place in Las Aguas neighborhood that aims to follow the principles of just urban transitions and to revitalize the city center sector (Universidad de los Andes, n.d.-b).

Fenicia involved a process of building knowledge by various faculties to solve one of the biggest problems of urban renewal worldwide, namely, gentrification (Pinilla & Arteaga, 2020). The influx of a wealthier population, such as students and faculty, increases demand for housing and commercial spaces near the campus, consequently impacting rental prices. This prompts investors to establish businesses and housing projects, potentially altering opportunities for low-income residents in the Fenicia neighborhood. While creating new job prospects and income opportunities, this shift might also displace households to more affordable areas in the city. To contribute to the solution of this challenge, Uniandes decided to participate in the articulation of the real estate transformation taking place in the center of Bogota to guarantee that the inhabitants of the neighborhood, could stay in the area highlighting their personal stories, community priorities and roots, and their integration into the urban transformation brought by the developments from a growing population associated with nine other universities in this sector of the city (Universidad de los Andes, n.d.-b). It aims to develop a participatory urban renewal decision-making process that strengthens the coordination and cooperation between current owners, potential investors, and the city government. The project seeks to achieve a sustainable coexistence based on joint work between all the actors involved in the project (Mejía & Caicedo, 2013). With Fenicia, Uniandes, hand in hand with the community, wants to achieve the improvement of the nine hectares renewal projects and to improve the living conditions of more than 400 families (Universidad de los Andes, n.d.-b). With these efforts, Fenicia becomes an epicenter for the creation of new ways of doing and exercising citizenship, cooperating, building, and understanding Bogota. Its purpose is to build a joint future with the highest spatial quality, where all the communities coexist: neighbors, university students, and visitors from the center of the city and enterprises.

Considering that we are halfway through the 2030 Agenda, and that all sectors should contribute to this Agenda to amplify its impact in the coming years, it could be interesting to consider the possibility of sharing the lessons learned and challenges faced in the Fenicia Program with other universities in the city center of Bogota. If universities like Universidad Jorge Tadeo Lozano, Universidad del Rosario, Universidad La Salle, and others were to join in working with their surrounding communities from a perspective of just urban transitions, the impact of these actions could easily be doubled or even tripled. This way, the academic sector's influence on fulfilling the Agenda could be significantly expanded tackling SDG 10 (reduced inequalities), SDG 11 (sustainable cities and communities), and SDG 17 (partnerships for the goals) in a direct way and supporting in an indirect way SDG 8 (decent work and economic growth) and SDG 4 (quality education) (Fig. 5.1).

Fig. 5.1. Timeline of Representative Milestones of Fenicia Program.
Source: Universidad de los Andes (n.d.-b).

The Sustainable Campus Strategy

The Universidad de los Andes (2022c) is committed to the environment through five areas that contribute to the analysis of the role of the University in sustainability and its contribution to the sustainable development of Bogota. These areas are: (I) culture and learning, (II) campus ecosystems, (III) climate change, (IV) campus operation, and (V) well-being and quality of life.

In relation to the campus ecosystem, the University has prioritized establishing green areas within its premises. These areas consist of 750 plant species, and by 2040, it is expected that 100% of these species will be native species. This strategy aims to conserve local biodiversity while establishing native tree cover that contributes to the reduction of greenhouse gas (GHG) emissions, the improvement of air quality on campus, and the promotion of well-being through the provision of a natural environment that promotes mental health and physical activity for the community (Universidad de los Andes, 2022c).

In 2022, an increase in the number of student organizations focused on sustainability was observed (Universidad de los Andes, 2022c). The impact of the activities implemented by these groups is highly valuable, as it extends beyond the campus and the Uniandes community, reaching families, friends, acquaintances, and local communities who are part of the city, and are crucial for sustainability efforts. As an example, the LixiLab project, which aims to improve the quality of life for farmers and crops in Mochuelo Alto (a rural area in the south of Bogota) by reducing soil and water pollution caused by heavy metals, through the implementation of a bioremediation biotechnology system (Universidad de los Andes, 2022c). This project is a clear example of how an initiative that emerges within the university has a significant impact on the city, contributing to advancing sustainable agriculture by pursuing cleaner production practices and addressing the restoration of soil and water quality in this rural ecosystem that is an actual part of the city (SDG 15: Life on land; and SDG 6: Clean water and sanitation).

Uniandes also has a strategy with a waste recovery process adapted and appropriate to the campus, achieving in the last two years a reduction of waste by 15% per person (Universidad de los Andes, 2022c). This has a major impact on ensuring SDG 12, which highlights the importance of responsible consumption and production. The sensibilization of topics such as sustainable consumption and responsible waste management in the community highlights the importance of recycling, reusing, and extending the useful life of materials impacting at the same time the consumption patterns of next generations. Because waste is one of the causes of the climate crisis (Universidad de los Andes, 2022c), it is important that higher education intuitions set an example to help achieve these needed changes as well as to encourage other sectors in society to implement effective and practical waste engagement solutions.

Apart from the initiatives mentioned, Uniandes is also committed to a strategy of responsible water consumption (Universidad de los Andes, 2022c). The water consumed on the Campus comes mainly from the city's aqueduct system, and another part comes from the treatment of rainwater collected in different campus buildings. These initiatives contribute directly to the achievement of SDG 6 (Clean water and sanitation), which calls for ensuring universal access to safe and affordable drinking water, sanitation, and hygiene. These actions have an influence on (i) improving water quality and (ii) the efficiency of water use as well as to keep strengthening a sustainable extraction strategy that guarantees the supply of fresh water in the city.

Finally, Uniandes also has made great efforts to be more efficient in energy consumption, regardless of the growth on the Campus. Moreover, over the past five years, Uniandes has achieved its goal of reducing GHG emissions by 22% by 2030, through a partnership with the energy marketer Celsia, which enabled the university to acquire most of its electricity consumption from renewable sources and avoid the emission of 500 tons of CO_2 during 2022 (Universidad de los Andes, 2022c).

This approach underscores Uniandes' status as an anchor institution, actively participating in initiatives that stimulate economic development, enhance community well-being, and expand educational opportunities, exemplifying the university's commitment to improve local and global societal outcomes (Birch et al., 2013). An illustrative case of this is the funding provided by the SDG Center for research examining the role of universities in achieving carbon neutrality through their teaching and practices, which serves as a prime example of why Uniandes is considered an anchor institution. This research, led by Jonathan Barton from the Pontifical Catholic University of Chile and supported by co-investigators from diverse institutions, including the National Polytechnic School of Ecuador, EAFIT University in Colombia, and the Massachusetts Institute of Technology, underscores the university's active participation in sustainability efforts

(Centro de los Objetivos de Desarrollo Sostenible para América Latina y el Caribe, 2023c).

The Uniandes campus consistently grapples with a range of challenges related to physical space, infrastructure, mobility, responsible resource utilization, and the effective management of daily-generated waste (Universidad de los Andes, 2022c). These challenges are closely intertwined with the goals of its Sustainability Program, which aspires to position Uniandes as a national and international leader in sustainable practices by strengthening eco-friendly activities and continually assessing and implementing best practices. While the campus has made significant progress in implementing various sustainability projects, initiatives, and management strategies, there are still numerous challenges and opportunities on the horizon. These sustainability efforts must address issues such as optimizing space utilization, enhancing infrastructure for improved environmental performance, upgrading transportation systems, and advancing waste management practices. As the University endeavors to set a benchmark on both the national and international stages, the journey toward a more sustainable campus is a continuous commitment that demands innovative solutions and unwavering dedication (Fig. 5.2).

The SDGs Center for Latin America and the Caribbean

The establishment of the SDG Center for Latin America and the Caribbean at Universidad de los Andes is explained by its academic tradition in social and environmental sustainability which is represented by various training and research programs on sustainable development and environment in different academic units. The SDG Center was created with the support of the SDSN, led by Professor Jeffrey Sachs.

Since its launch in September 2018, the SDG Center has sought to create research and quality evidence-based information to contribute to sustainable development and support the achievement of the 2030 Agenda in alliance with universities of excellence, companies, governments, and civil society organizations in Colombia and Latin America and the Caribbean. To achieve its objective, the SDG

Fig. 5.2. Timeline of Representative Milestones of Sustainable Campus.

Sources: Universidad de los Andes (2021a, 2022a, 2022c).

Center has it focused on these three themes that are pressing challenges that the region face: reduction of inequalities and poverty relief; conservation of biodiversity; and mitigation and adaptation to climate change.

In this sense, the Center has worked to build a regional research network for sustainable development which aims to connect existing efforts within Uniandes and partner universities with the purpose of contributing to the generation of knowledge for the achievement of the SDGs in Latin America and the Caribbean. To support this objective, four international seminars were held to create alliances and academic networks between researchers, universities, and think tanks in Latin America and the Caribbean. In each of the seminars, a call was launched to encourage joint analysis work between researchers from Latin American and Caribbean universities and research centers. This effort aimed to finance interdisciplinary and regional research that contributed to the production of new knowledge for the achievement of the SDGs. Table 5.1 presents the research projects funded by the SDG Center.

The SDG Center also aims to become a knowledge hub that contributes to the education of the next generation of leaders of the region. Indeed, since 2019, the SDG Center has been working on a portfolio of courses and public lectures on sustainable development. This portfolio includes face to face and virtual courses that aim to address the needs of university students and a wider audience, including decisionmakers, managers, civil society, school teachers, and in general anyone with an interest in understanding the SDGs from a regional perspective. The portfolio counts formal and non-formal products of education such as tailor-made courses for enterprises, open lectures, Massive Online Open Courses (MOOC), and basic cycles courses. All the educational offer of the Center has a multidisciplinary and transversal perspective since it approaches sustainable development from different knowledge areas (Universidad Politécnica de Madrid, n.d.). The Center achieved to impact around 500 students of Uniandes and had more than 25,000 thousand students globally with its MOOC's.

The SDG Center serves as a vital knowledge hub, playing a pivotal role in the creation, distribution, and application of knowledge pertaining to sustainable development goals. Operating in alignment with the concept of "ecologies of intermediation," the Center acts as a catalyst for fostering coordination and collaboration among a wide array of stakeholders, which includes researchers, policymakers, and civil society organizations (Soberón et al., 2022). Through extensive research endeavors, the Center promotes comprehensive collaboration across various disciplines within the realms of natural, economic, and social sciences, significantly bolstering the foundational knowledge required to drive sustainable transitions. This interconnected and interdisciplinary approach not only aids in managing the intricacies of sustainability transitions

Table 5.1. Research Projects Funded by the SDG Center.

Prioritized SDG	Research Project Title	Universities Involved
SDG 11: (Sustainable cities and communities)	"Urban wetlands in Latin America: a solution for sustainable cities SDG 11"	• Pontificia Universidad Católica de Chile, Chile • Universidad del Norte, Colombia • Pontificia Universidad Católica de Perú, Perú
	"Transport and equity: addressing accessibility in urban margins"	• Pontificia Universidad Católica de Chile, Chile • Universidad de los Andes, Colombia • Associação Nacional de Transportes Públicos, Brazil • Universidad del Norte, Colombia • World Resources Institute, USA
SDG 2 (Zero hunger) and SDG 15 (Life on land)	"Sustainability and development in the territories: A systemic and local look at the achievement of rural landscapes and sustainable food production systems"	• Pontificia Universidad Javieriana, Colombia • Centro Interdisciplinario de Investigación para el Desarrollo Integral Regional CIIDIR Unidad Oaxaca, Mexico
	"Enhancement of the top predators (jaguar and puma) of Latin America and compensation mechanism for ranchers in order to guarantee the conservation of biodiversity and economic subsistence of small producers on a regional scale"	• Pontificia Universidad Católica de Chile, Chile • Universidad Nacional Autónoma de México, Mexico

SDG 13 (Climate action)	"Multistakeholder action as a central axis to work towards mitigation and climate change in a post pandemic era"	• Universidad EAFIT, Colombia • Pontificia Universidad Católica de Chile, Chile • Universidad Privada Boliviana, Bolivia • Universidad de Monterrey, Mexico • Fundação Getulio Vargas, Brasil • Pontificia Universidad Católica de Perú, Perú • University of the West Indies, Jamaica
	"Carbon neutrality: Learning and action strategies in Latin America universities"	• Pontificia Universidad Católica de Chile, Chile • Escuela Politénica Nacional, Ecuador • Universidad EAFIT, Colombia • Massachusetts Institute of Technology, USA

Sources: Centro de los Objetivos de Desarrollo Sostenible para América Latina y el Caribe (2020, 2022a, 2022b, 2023c, 2023a, 2023b).

but also nurtures collaborative relationships, trust, and mutual support, even in the face of differences and conflicts. Ultimately, it propels collective progress toward the realization of the SDGs.

The SDG Center also seeks to monitor and analyze policies and programs to contribute to the global discussions on the implementation of policies aiming to achieve the 2030 Agenda, and to illustrate those policies using examples from the region. One of its strategic products is the SDG Index for Latin America and the Caribbean, which is based on the methodology of the global index created by SDSN and the Bertelsmann Stiftundg (Schmidt-Traub et al., 2017; Sustainable Development Solutions Network, 2017).

Several valuable insights emerged during the establishment of the Center. Firstly, the creation of an expert committee comprising academics from diverse disciplines proved instrumental in shaping the agenda and strategic directions of the Center. Additionally, establishing strategic partnerships with regional allies who not only endorsed the Center's initiatives but also actively engaged in project proposals greatly enhanced the visibility of CODS at the regional level.

Furthermore, it is worth noting that while prioritizing specific SDGs is crucial for focused efforts, an even more effective approach involves concentrating on the most pressing challenges confronting the region. These challenges should be amenable to interdisciplinary solutions, with both direct and indirect interactions, fostering synergies across multiple SDGs.

Uniandes and Its Contribution to the 2030 Agenda Through Philanthropy

Based on the words of Rector Raquel Bernal in the philanthropy (Universidad de los Andes, 2022b), it can be inferred that Uniandes is actively involved in promoting the SDGs through its mission and philanthropic funds with the establishment of various public–private alliances. With innovative alliances that count on high visibility, companies, and other organizations such as Uniandes can achieve their objectives in terms of social responsibility, while helping to meet the most urgent needs in the country. Philanthropic activity transcends the conventional concept of solidarity to increasingly establish itself as an instrument of transversal policies that range from development aid, in favor of education, health, and against poverty in disadvantaged countries, to the promotion of art and culture, scientific research or sustainability (Universidad de los Andes, n.d.-a). Uniandes offers a unique combination of reputation, relationships, and resources such as grants, operational programs, and impact investments to strengthen the mission of the institution and the SDGs can be fulfilled involving different actors.

Through numerous philanthropic efforts, Uniandes creates opportunities to increase access to high quality education and permanence of students from different socioeconomic backgrounds. With these programs, the University aims to transform and innovate the curriculum as well as actively cooperate in the development of the country with education for all with programs such as "Quiero Estudiar," "Quiero Enseñar, "Pa'lante Pacífico," "Pa'lante Caribe," "Vamos Pa'lante," and initiatives such as "Necesitamos Pensar," which offer scholarships and financial aid to students from different regions of the country (Universidad de los Andes, 2022b). All these programs are framed in different SDGs: (i) SDG 4, which is "to guarantee inclusive and quality education for all and promote lifelong learning." It sets as its goal the "substantial expansion" of the number of scholarships available for enrollment in higher education. (ii) SDG 10 "Reduction of inequalities" by increasing opportunities to access education and inclusion of students in vulnerable situations, which has an indirect impact on economic growth leading to better jobs (SDG 8) and a better quality of life (SDG 3). (iii) SDG 17 "Partnerships to achieve the objectives," because thanks to public–private alliances resources have been obtained to support students across the country (United Nations, 2015).

Philanthropic campaigns at Uniandes achieved between 2016 and 2021 30,725,191.82 USD (Universidad de los Andes, 2022b) that contributed to the implementation and the achievement of the goals settled by the 2030 Agenda as well as to strengthen its commitment toward the transformation and development of the country based on education and innovation, through, for example, providing financial support and funding for the studies of 439 students during 2021 (Universidad de los Andes, 2022b). As an advocate, Uniandes supports awareness through integrating the SDGs into its programs, efforts, and leadership, seeking to be drivers of impact, catalyzing change and generating impact.

In summary, Uniandes is actively engaged in the Collaborative Value Creation Framework as Austin and Seitanidi (2012) define it, a framework that emphasizes the importance of partnering processes, value creation dynamics, and collaboration outcomes. In this context, the University is committed to generating collaborative efforts with public and private organizations to promote the SDGs. These collaborations represent the partnering processes that aim to co-create value for various stakeholders, such as students, society, and the environment. The philanthropic campaigns and alliances with high-visibility companies illustrate how Uniandes is involved in value creation dynamics, where economic, social, and environmental value is being generated.

Universidad de los Andes and Its Contribution to the Mobility of the City

Uniandes has actively proposed multiple initiatives to address the diverse needs and challenges associated with urban mobility. In 2009, the Faculty of Engineering created the Urban and Regional Sustainability Studies Group (SUR) to generate novel knowledge and contribute to the comprehension and resolution of transportation, mobility, urban, and welfare issues, with a strong emphasis on innovation and sustainability (Grupo de Estudios en Sostenibilidad Urbana y Regional, n.d.). These endeavors play a crucial role in reinforcing Uniandes' position as an anchor institution and exemplify the University's deep-rooted connections with the local community and the city (Birch et al., 2013). In its role as an anchor institution, Uniandes plays a pivotal role in championing initiatives designed to improve urban mobility in the city. This commitment extends beyond the well-being of its own university community;

it also serves the greater good by contributing to the welfare of the city's residents and the overall sustainability of the city's transportation system.

The Uniandina Mobility Survey, together with the Regularization and Management Plan, laid the foundations for the construction of the Sustainable Mobility Plan, which establishes three pillars (Bocarejo et al., 2012; Rodríguez et al., 2020). The first pillar is related to the transformation of the university's environment, prioritizing pedestrian flows, and promoting traffic planning designs. The second pillar is to stimulate the use of bicycles by improving bicycle parking infrastructure and increasing access to bicycles through a rental system and a purchase scheme (for 2022, the university had 627 bicycle parking spaces). Additionally, it seeks to encourage the use of carpooling to substantially increase the occupancy rate of vehicles (Grupo de Estudios en Sostenibilidad Urbana y Regional & Gerencia del Campus Universidad de los Andes, n.d.). Finally, the university had 16 free spots for 100% electric cars, aiming to promote this mode of transportation in 2022 (Universidad de los Andes, 2022c).

Another initiative where Uniandes participates is the "day without car." This is an initiative promoted by the local government and aims to contribute to the environment, promoting the use of public transport, cycling, and encouraging people to engage in physical activity. Even though this is a district initiative, due to the close relationship of the SUR group with district mobility projects, the university has joined and promoted it from its origins (Grupo de Estudios en Sostenibilidad Urbana y Regional, n.d.; Universidad de los Andes, 2022c). All the initiatives presented contribute to the sustainability of the city and to the achievement of the SDGs in diverse ways. The incentives for bicycle use contribute to the fulfillment of SDG 3 (Good health and well-being), by encouraging physical activity that promotes physical and mental health. In addition, the initiative to increase bicycle access is related to SDG 10 (Reduced inequalities), as it is designed to ease the sale of bicycles through financing schemes for lower-income members of the community. Together, the initiatives presented contribute to the attainment of SDG 11 (Sustainable cities and communities),

SDG 13 (Climate action), and SDG 9 (Industry innovation and infrastructure), as they promote more efficient forms of transports such as electric mobility that reduce GHG emissions, traffic congestion, and encourage the development of infrastructure and platforms for the organization and coordination of shared trips.

One of the SUR group's initiatives that is worth highlighting is "Conduce a 50 vive al 100." The project seeks to include speed management on the country's roads as a crosscutting component of a bill to the Congress of the Republic in order to save lives on the road and establish limits that are compatible with activities intrinsic to urban environments such as walking, cycling, and using public spaces (Ortiz, 2022), which are essential for the fulfillment of SDG 3 (Good health and well-being) and SDG 11 (Sustainable cities and communities) (Grupo de Estudios en Sostenibilidad Urbana y Regional, 2021).

Uniandes and Its Support to the City and the Community to Respond to the Challenge of the Pandemic of COVID-19

Covida was a project implemented by the Universidad de los Andes, from 18 April 2020 to 29 March 2021. The main objective was to process free tests to diagnose SAR-CoV-2 in people without symptoms or with mild symptoms and who, due to their profession or high mobility presented a greater risk of infection or of infecting others. Covida was the first project where a university became part of the Public Health Surveillance System. The project was the only project that contemplated sampling asymptomatic people during the first year of the pandemic in Colombia (Diaz, 2023).

To fulfill its objective, Covida collected samples from individuals at home, also from taxi drivers, and pedestrians. In addition, it created follow-up processes for contacts of individuals who tested positive, to reduce the number of infected people. In total, during the duration of the Covida project, more than 65,000 tests were taken (Diaz, 2023; Varela et al., 2021). Additionally, to the main objective of Covida, the Universidad de los Andes aimed to put the science and capacity of the university at the service of the community.

After the closure of the first stage of the Covida project, a second stage was implemented, which was the Covida strategy "The vaccine belongs to everyone." This process lasted 75 days with the inoculation of more than 110,000 doses of vaccines. This process was implemented in three localities in Bogota (Bosa, Usme, and Ciudad Bolivar).

Covida, being an academic project that aimed to support the response to the epidemiological emergency of the COVID-19 pandemic, contributed directly to the fulfillment of the SDG 3: Health and well-being, and also indirectly to reduce the negative impact of the pandemic on Colombian households (SDG 10: Reduced inequalities) through strengthening relations in between different stakeholders (SDG 17: Partnerships for the goals). This was a strategy of great importance during the pandemic, where the Universidad de los Andes shows its leadership and the importance of the social well-being of the community, this highlights how the Universidad de los Andes contributes to the sustainable development (Diaz, 2023; Varela et al., 2021).

The Covida project serves as a prominent example of Universidad de los Andes' role as an anchor institution due to its extensive involvement in addressing community needs during the COVID-19 pandemic. This initiative went beyond the typical boundaries of academia, becoming an integral part of the Public Health System. Through close collaboration with various private and public organizations and institutions, Uniandes showcased its unwavering commitment to community health, the reduction of inequalities, and the enhancement of overall well-being. By actively engaging with the complex challenges presented by the pandemic, Covida highlighted the university's pivotal role in improving public health and society at large, thereby solidifying its position as a dedicated anchor institution (Birch et al., 2013).

Table 5.2 presents a summary of the strategies implemented by the University and how those are related to the Sustainable Development Agenda.

Table 5.2. Summary of Some Contributions of Uniandes Initiatives to the SDGs.

Initiative	SDG	Contributions
Fenicia program	SDG 10: Reduced inequalities	Addressing urban inequalities and preserving cultural identity while mitigating gentrification
	SDG 11: Sustainable Cities and Communities	Encouraging a sustainable city center and coexistence among diverse stakeholders
	SDG 17: Partnerships for the goals	Exemplifying the importance of collaborative partnerships for urban transformation
	SDG 8: Decent work and economic growth	Driving sustainable economic growth through job creation and attracting investors
	SDG 4: Quality education	Fostering collaboration between universities and the local community to enhance education
Sustainable campus	SDG 11: Sustainable cities and communities	Improving the quality of life on campus and promoting sustainable practices
	SDG 12: Responsible consumption and production	Directly supporting SDG 12 through responsible consumption and production
	SDG 6: Clean water and sanitation	Promoting efficient water use and sustainable extraction strategies
	SDG 7: Affordable and clean energy	Goals for reducing GHG emissions, utilizing renewable energy, and installing solar panels
	SDG 15: Life on land	Establishing native green areas to conserve biodiversity and promote sustainable land management

Philanthropy	SDG 4: Quality education	Expanding access to quality education through different programs
	SDG 10: Reduced inequalities	Reducing inequalities in education access through scholarships and financial aid
	SDG 17: Partnerships for the goals	Collaborating with public and private organizations in philanthropic campaigns
Mobility	SDG 3: Good health and well-being	Mobility initiatives promoting walking, cycling, and reducing traffic speed
	SDG 9: Industry, innovation, and infrastructure	Contributing to sustainable infrastructure development
	SDG 10: Reduced inequalities	Facilitating access to bicycles for lower-income community members
	SDG 11: Sustainable cities and communities	Promotion of sustainable mobility, traffic speed reduction, and other initiatives contributes to more sustainable cities and safer, healthier communities
	SDG 13: Climate action	Promoting cleaner transportation for climate action
Covida	SDG 3: Good health and well-being	Providing SAR-CoV-2 testing for those without symptoms
	SDG 10: Reduced inequalities	Enhancing equitable access to testing and reducing health disparities
	SDG 17: Partnerships for the goals	Collaborating with multiple stakeholders in pandemic response and vaccination efforts

CONCLUSIONS

Uniandes as an academic institution has had an important contribution to the achievement of the Sustainable Development Agenda in Bogota, and in Colombia. This contribution has been made through research projects, academic, and social activities, including the conservation of local environments and the creation of green areas in the main campus, as the conservation of water, electricity, and the work with communities and addressing the challenges of gentrification around its campus. In addition, Uniandes has implemented and participated in different campaigns and initiatives whose main objective is to promote the health and well-being of individuals and society and have an important impact on the sustainable development of the country.

The University also faces forthcoming challenges concerning the education of its students and faculty, as well as the integration of these efforts into a vast network of universities, both domestically and internationally. The existing knowledge level among these academic communities regarding the SDG underscores the imperative to enhance pedagogical strategies to increase awareness about the impending challenges related to the 2030 Agenda. Uniandes, being one of the foremost institutions in the region, should bolster its endeavors to foster a community of experts and students in various higher education institutions, amplifying its influence on local, regional, and global scales.

Simultaneously, the ongoing discussions about reevaluating the 2030 Agenda and engaging in post-SDGs dialogues present a challenge for a university committed to these objectives while remaining receptive to policy and academic deliberations in a post-pandemic world. The mounting frequency of extreme events linked to climate change further necessitates a reevaluation of priorities. Encouraging dialogues with the private sector, social organizations, public sector, and academia could prove invaluable in uncovering innovative solutions to the societal challenges with an unwavering commitment to the goal of leaving no one behind.

REFERENCES

Austin, J. E., & Seitanidi, M. M. (2012). Collaborative value creation: A review of partnering between nonprofits and businesses. Part 2: Partnership processes and outcomes. *Nonprofit and Voluntary Sector Quarterly*, *41*(6), 929–968.

Benneworth, P., Charles, D., & Madanipour, A. (2010). Building localized interactions between universities and cities through university spatial development. *European Planning Studies*, *18*(10), 1611–1629. https://doi.org/10.1080/09654313.2010.5043

Birch, E., Perry, D. C., & Taylor, H. L., Jr. (2013). Universities as anchor institutions. *Journal of Higher Education Outreach and Engagement*, *17*, 7–16.

Bocarejo, J. P., Rodríguez, Á., Delgadillo, H. C., Caicedo, A. M., Escobar, D., Garzón, M., Pérez, M. A., Sáenz, D., & Tovar, S. R. (2012). *Actualización del Plan de Regularización y Manejo de la Universidad de los Andes*. https://linkprotect.cudasvc.com/url?a=https%3a%2f%2fsostenibilidad.uniandes.edu.co%2fmovilidad%2fen-uniandes&c=E,1,N6LsjBcHtdkaIpWvc2tyPFopEAyBvZZLRgwKHULLSJmBXH6yOzNep257CCcl_DhP0AnY3FJ5Ezbvrkqk2LDL9ZzhOiNRlrgFyCTJV8qGEDjoRR4,&typo=1

Centro de los Objetivos de Desarrollo Sostenible para América Latina y el Caribe. (2020). *El centro ODS presenta el Seminario Internacional de humedales urbanos en Latinoamerica*. https://cods.uniandes.edu.co/el-centro-ods-presenta-el-seminario-internacional-de-humedales-urbanos-en-latinoamerica/

Centro de los Objetivos de Desarrollo Sostenible para América Latina y el Caribe. (2022a). *Cooperación "Multi-Actor", clave para cumplir con el ODS 13*. https://cods.uniandes.edu.co/cooperacion-multi-actor-clave-para-cumplir-con-el-ods-13/

Centro de los Objetivos de Desarrollo Sostenible para América Latina y el Caribe. (2022b). *Transporte y equidad: abordando la accesibilidad en los márgenes urbanos*. https://cods.uniandes.edu.co/transporte-y-equidad-abordando-la-accesibilidad-en-los-margenes-urbanos/

Centro de los Objetivos de Desarrollo Sostenible para América Latina y el Caribe. (2023a). *Desarrollo (in)sostenible en territorios rurales de América Latina*. https://cods.uniandes.edu.co/desarrollo-insostenible-en-territorios-rurales-de-america-latina/

Centro de los Objetivos de Desarrollo Sostenible para América Latina y el Caribe. (2023b). *La convervación del puma y del jaguar en el contexto de los objetivos de desarrollo sostenible en latinoamérica*. https://cods.uniandes.edu.co/la-conservacion-del-puma-y-del-jaguar-en-el-contexto-de-los-objetivos-de-desarrollo-sostenible-en-latinoamerica/

Centro de los Objetivos de Desarrollo Sostenible para América Latina y el Caribe. (2023c). *Las instituciones de enseñanza superior juegan un rol fundamental en la respuesta al cambio climático*. https://cods.uniandes.edu.co/las-instituciones-de-ensenanza-superior-juegan-un-rol-fundamental-en-la-respuesta-al-cambio-climatico/

Diaz, A. (2023). *Tiempos de epidemia. Tres emergencias sanitarias en Bogotá: 1840, 1918, 2020*. Publicaciones Uniandes.

Grupo de Estudios en Sostenibilidad Urbana y Regional. (n.d.). *Grupo de Estudios en Sostenibilidad Urbana y Regional SUR*. https://sur.uniandes.edu.co/

Grupo de Estudios en Sostenibilidad Urbana y Regional, & Gerencia del Campus Universidad de los Andes. (n.d.). *Manual de Movilidad Universidad de los Andes*. https://programas.uniandes.edu.co/articulo/movilidad-sostenible-posgrado

Grupo de Estudios en Sostenibilidad Urbana y Regional. (2021). *Conduce a 50 vive al 100*. https://www.conducea50.com/

Hughes, S., & Hoffmann, M. (2020). Just urban transitions: Toward a research agenda. *Wiley Interdisciplinary Reviews: Climate Change, 11*(3), e640.

Mejía, C., & Caicedo, V. (2013). Urban design with an inclusive vision: The Los Andes University challenge with a growth model. *Dearq Uniandes, 13*, 24–37.

Ortiz, J. (2022). *Ley Julián Esteban busca reducir siniestros viales*. https://uniandes.edu.co/es/noticias/ingenieria/ley-julian-esteban-busca-reducir-siniestros-viales#:~=M%C3%A1s%20de%207.000%20personas%20perdieron,Andes%2C%20busca%20reducir%20esta%20cifra

Pinilla, J. F., & Arteaga, M. (2020). Governance through Conflict: Consensus building in the Fenicia Urban Renewal Project in Bogotá, Colombia. *Built Environment*, 47(01), 31–55.

Rodríguez, Á., Vinasco, C., & Mesa, S. (2020). *Encuesta de Movilidad Uniandina*. https://sostenibilidad.uniandes.edu.co/movilidad/en-uniandes

Schmidt-Traub, G., Kroll, C., Teksoz, K., Durand-Delacre, D., & Sachs, J. D. (2017). National baselines for the sustainable development goals assessed in the SDG index and dashboards. *Nature Geoscience*, 10(8), 547–555. https://doi.org/10.1038/ngeo2985

Soberón, M., Sánchez-Chaparro, T., Smith, A., Moreno-Serna, J., Oquendo-Di Cosola, V., & Mataix, C. (2022). Exploring the possibilities for deliberately cultivating more effective ecologies of Intermediation. *Environmental Innovation and Societal Transitions*, 44, 125–144. https://doi.org/10.1016/j.eist.2022.06.003

Sustainable Development Solutions Network. (2017). *Global responsibilities*. https://www.jstor.org/stable/pdf/resrep15870.6.pdf

Sustainable Development Solutions Network. (2020). *Accelerating education for the SDGs in universities: A guide for universities, colleges, and tertiary and higher education institutions*. https://resources.unsdsn.org/accelerating-education-for-the-sdgs-in-universities-a-guide-for-universities-colleges-and-tertiary-and-higher-education-institutions

Times Higher Education. (2022). *Times Higher Education impact ranking 2022*. https://www.timeshighereducation.com/impactrankings

UI Green Metric. (2022). *UI Green Metric*. https://greenmetric.ui.ac.id/

Universidad de los Andes. (n.d.-a). *Dirección de Filantropía*. https://donaciones.uniandes.edu.co/donaciones/proposito/descubre-una-causa

Universidad de los Andes. (n.d.-b). *Historia Programa Progresa Fenicia*. https://progresafenicia.uniandes.edu.co/

Universidad de los Andes. (n.d.-c). *Misión Universidad de los Andes*. https://uniandes.edu.co/es/universidad/informacion-general/mision

Universidad de los Andes. (2021a). *Plan de Sostenibilidad 2021–2025*. https://sostenibilidad.uniandes.edu.co/images/Documentos/PLAN-DE-SOSTENIBILIDAD.pdf

Universidad de los Andes. (2021b). *Programa de Desarrollo Integral 2021–2025*. https://uniandes.edu.co/es/noticias/en-el-campus/los-andes-presenta-su-programa-de-desarrollo-integral-20212025

Universidad de los Andes. (2022a). *Conversión de Energía*. https://mecanica.uniandes.edu.co/es/grupos-de-investigacion/conversion-de-energia.

Universidad de los Andes. (2022b). *Informe de Filantropía 2021*. https://donaciones.uniandes.edu.co/sites/default/files/informe_filantropia_2021_0.pdf

Universidad de los Andes. (2022c). *Reporte de Sostenibilidad 2022*. https://sostenibilidad.uniandes.edu.co/indicadores-de-sostenibilidad

Universidad Politécnica de Madrid. (n.d.). *Education as a strategic line of the SDG Center for Latin America and the Caribbean*. https://blogs.upm.es/education4sdg/2021/09/15/education-as-a-strategic-line-of-the-sdg-center-for-latin-america-and-the-caribbean/

United Nations. (2015). *Transforming our world: The 2030 agenda for sustainable development*. Resolution Adopted by the General Assembly on 25 September 2015. https://sdgs.un.org/2030agenda

Valero, A., & Van Reenen, J. (2018). The economic impact of universities: Evidence from across the globe. *Economics of Education Review*, 68, 53–67. https://doi.org/10.1016/j.econedurev.2018

Varela, A. R., Florez, L. J. H., Tamayo-Cabeza, G., Contreras-Arrieta, S., Restrepo, S. R., Laajaj, R., Gutierrez, G. B., Guevara, Y. P. R., Caballero-Díaz, Y., Florez, M. V., Osorio, E., Barbieri, I. S., Sanchez, D. R., Nuñez, L. L., Bernal, R., Oliveros, S. R., Zapata, L. S., Guevara-Suarez, M., Uribe, A. G., & Behrentz, E. (2021). Factors associated with SARS-CoV-2 infection in Bogotá, Colombia: Results from a large epidemiological surveillance study. *The Lancet Regional Health – Americas*, 2, 100048. https://doi.org/10.1016/j.lana.2021.100048

NOTES FOR CHAPTER AUTHOR

Note that as a part of the SDG Center, the contribution to education for sustainability part of the blog on SDG 4 published by Universidad Politécnica de Madrid was used (https://blogs.upm.es/education4sdg/2021/09/15/education-as-a-strategic-line-of-the-sdg-center-for-latin-america-and-the-caribbean/).

6

THE ROLE OF HIGHER EDUCATION INSTITUTIONS IN URBAN CLIMATE TRANSFORMATION

John Cleveland and Azanta Thakur

Boston Green Ribbon Commission, USA

ABSTRACT

To achieve their climate goals for net zero emissions and long-term resilience, most cities will need to radically transform their core urban systems of transportation, energy, waste, buildings, and stormwater management, among others. Multiple billions of dollars will have to be invested by the public and private sectors, and governance structures for planning, regulation, and decision-making will need to be restructured to rapidly adapt to changing climate demands. Higher education institutions can play a unique role in informing, facilitating, and accelerating this transformation. Their research knowledge can inform investments and regulatory decision-making; their students can provide the critical skills needed by private and public stakeholders to support implementation; their campuses can act as "living labs" to test out innovative climate solutions; and their political influence can help inform and advance needed public policy changes. The Boston Green

Ribbon Commission (GRC) is a CEO network whose mission is to accelerate the implementation of the City's Climate Action Plan by convening, organizing, and enabling leaders from Boston's key sectors, including higher education. Boston and its metro surroundings have one of the highest concentrations of higher education institutions in the world. There are over 64 colleges and universities in Boston and neighboring Cambridge alone, many of which are members of the GRC's Higher Education Working Group (HEWG). This chapter will share the lessons learned from the GRC and the HEWG on how higher education institutions can help convene key stakeholders to accelerate the urban transformation needed to achieve ambitious climate goals.

Keywords: Climate change; climate action; higher education; mitigation; decarbonization; resilience; urban transformation; collaboration

HOW CITY CLIMATE AMBITIONS ARE DRIVING GLOBAL URBAN TRANSFORMATION

The City of Boston is now committed to 100% community-wide carbon neutrality by 2050 and long-term resilience against the climate risks of coastal flooding, extreme storms, and extreme heat (City of Boston, 2022a). It is part of a network of hundreds of global cities that are setting increasingly bold and aggressive climate goals that will require serious transformation of multiple core urban systems. These commitments to change are driving a new urban model that alters the way cities design and use physical space, generate economic wealth, consume, and dispose of resources, exploit and sustain the natural ecosystems they need, and prepare for the future.

These pioneering cities are trying, in just a few decades, to eliminate fossil fuels from their immense, complex systems of energy supply, transportation, buildings, and waste management. Just as systematically and rapidly, they are preparing their built infrastructures, ecosystems, economies, and residents to handle the grave impacts of extreme storms, rainfall, heat, drought, and rising seas – conditions already experienced by many cities and projected to get much, much worse (City of Boston, 2016a).

Climate leadership cities are innovating aggressively and radically – by developing and implementing experimental projects, tackling entire urban systems, and reweaving the physical and cultural fabric of the entire city (City of Boston, 2016b). These ideas contain the seeds of a new urban paradigm that is reshaping what people think a city can and should become. They introduce new ways for cities to compete successfully in a global 21st century economy that is shifting to renewable energy. They herald new ways for cities to more efficiently use the vast quantities of energy and materials they need. They announce new ways for cities to value and obtain the benefits their wetlands, forestlands, open space, and other ecosystems provide. They signal new ways for cities to develop the social and physical adaptability needed to anticipate and prepare for uncertain future conditions.

This is not the first time cities have transformed themselves to adapt to new circumstances. Since cities were invented some 6,000 years ago, they have often fundamentally evolved in response to war and conquest, trade and technologies, earthquakes, and other natural disasters, as well as demographic shifts, socioeconomic reforms, and political revolutions (Thorns, 2017). But this time, it is climate change that is driving a full-scale evolution.

The new urban model is still in an early stage of emergence. Its elements have not yet been fully defined and assembled into a coherent practice by cities. It has not yet locked in as the comprehensive new way of doing business in cities, and it faces considerable obstacles. The fossil-fuel sector continues strenuous political resistance to sweeping changes and many national and state-level governments have failed to pursue sensible policies. Cities have limited control over many factors needed to implement radical innovations. Many city residents are reluctant to embrace changes that alter their lifestyles or cost them more money and other residents suffer from a system that was made to work against them or without them in mind. Even the most forward-looking and capable cities struggle sometimes to develop the technical competencies, financial capital, social progress, and community constituencies needed to move forward aggressively.

But it is clear that because of climate change, cities around the world will be different at the end of the 21st century. Whether they will be prosperous, healthy, safe, equitable, and better places for everyone to live in, remains to be seen. There's no guarantee that a climate-driven transformation will occur fully in all cities or many cities or even just a few cities. But a possible future city, a radically different city than the modern one we know, is coming into view. It is emerging in cities all around us, in the cities that have decided to turn the climate disaster into an opportunity, cities that are making the urban future now.

Urban institutions of higher education are poised to play a critical and catalytic role in this transformation (Rantz, 2002).

Cities and heavily populated urban areas are tasked with simultaneously addressing disaster reduction, urban resilience, and adaptation as well as urban poverty. Many higher education institutions are situated in historically low-income or minority–majority communities, paving the way for both indirect and direct impacts for those experiencing pre-existing vulnerability to the effects of climate change. An example of this is seen in Boston University School of Public Health's research in Chelsea, Massachusetts – also addressed below (Milando et al., 2022). Higher education institutions have the unique ability to assist cities in the urban climate transformation due to their distinctive campuses, student body, faculty capabilities, and research labs. Many universities are also mapping the effects and models of climate change, further research to sustain city work and further prepare residents for realistic understandings of the changes happening in their city. Not only is higher education an agent for sustainable development and urban transformation, but it is also the pathway forward. This chapter examines how a city such as Boston has benefited from the collaboration of several higher education institutions.

THE ROLE OF THE GRC IN BOSTON'S CLIMATE TRANSFORMATION

The GRC was created in 2010 in response to two key developments. The first was the 2009 creation of the City's first serious climate action plan. Well over a year in the making and involving input from a robust set of community stakeholders, "Sparking Boston's Climate Revolution" set a goal of a 25% reduction in greenhouse gas (GHG) emissions by 2020 (City of Boston, 2010). In 2019, the City increased this commitment to a 100% GHG reduction by 2050.

The second development was a five-year, $50 million commitment in 2009 from the Barr Foundation, the City's largest independent foundation, to climate change grantmaking, making it one of the largest climate funders in the country at the time.[1] After conversations between one of the Barr Foundation's founders, Amos Hostetter, and then-Mayor Thomas Menino,[2] it became clear that achieving the City's climate goal would eventually indeed require a "revolution" – transformational redesign of multiple core urban systems. A sampling of these daunting challenges includes the following:

- Completely decarbonizing the City's electricity grid.
- Eliminating the use of fossil fuels for thermal services.
- Implementing energy efficiency retrofits in all the City's 82,000 buildings.
- Electrifying all modes of transportation (light duty, medium/heavy duty, transit, and boats/shipping).
- Radically increasing the use of active transportation modes (biking and walking).
- Achieving zero waste citywide.
- Building coastal protections along Boston's entire 47-mile coastline.
- Radically increasing green infrastructure for flood control.
- Making every neighborhood resilient to extreme heat events.

These changes would require enormous effort, capital, and simultaneous social and political will. With the City controlling less than 3% of total urban land and emissions, it became clear that the transformation could not happen without deep and committed support from the City's civic and business leadership (City of Boston, 2022a). The question was, who would convene these leaders to understand, support, and help implement this transformation? Out of this dialogue emerged the GRC, with the mission to "Accelerate the implementation of the City's Climate Action Plan by convening, organizing, and enabling leaders from Boston's key sectors" (Boston Green Ribbon Commission, 2023a).

GRC membership is made up of dozens of the City's top leaders – from universities, utilities, hospitals, financial institutions, real estate organizations, and nonprofits – who are committed to organization-level climate action to meet the City's carbon neutral targets and other climate goals (Boston Green Ribbon Commission, 2023a). The GRC membership also includes key agency heads from the City of Boston and Commonwealth of Massachusetts. Private sector members represent large, place-based institutions and businesses that are deeply intertwined with the economy, talent, culture, and history of Boston. Most are long-term asset owners with strong reputations for leadership who understand that their future, and Boston's, depends on viable strategies for thriving in a rapidly changing climate.

The GRC's hallmark is its ability to convene across sectors to tackle complex problems in a neutral room. Organized as a completely voluntary leadership network,[3] the GRC uses a combination of strategic advising, leading by example, implementation support and advocacy to support of the following city climate priorities:

- *Advance climate justice* – Assure that climate justice is acknowledged as a priority, widely understood, and measurably advanced through programs and projects that address it systemically.

- *Strengthen climate resilience* – Support the creation of governance structures, financing mechanisms, and regulatory requirements to manage the resilience investments needed to ensure a safe and climate-resilient Boston.

- *Accelerate carbon mitigation* – Assure that the City of Boston reaches its interim GHG reduction targets and has in place the necessary regulatory structure to be on a pathway to carbon neutrality by 2050.

- *Encourage more informed and activated residents* – Support Boston residents, neighborhoods, and organizations to be more proactive on climate change – informed and aware, prepared and connected, and engaged and creative.

The GRC is funded by its members, most of whom make annual tax-deductible contributions to the operating budget as well as occasional contributions to special projects as they arise.[4] Additional support comes from foundations and individuals. The GRC is not a separate non-profit entity. A national non-profit that has worked for over a decade with cities on their climate strategies – the Innovation Network for Communities – serves as the fiscal agent for the GRC. They accept contributions from donors, pay invoices, and manage all tax and reporting responsibilities for the Commission.

The Commission has five sector-based and issue-based working groups – Commercial Real Estate, Cultural Institutions, Health Care, Higher Education, and Coastal Resilience (Boston Green Ribbon Commission, 2023a). These working groups bring together prominent leaders to share their market-based realities and weigh in on important policy directions for climate action in addition to learning about technical and managerial best practices from their peers. Members regularly share their strategies and experiences with the Mayor, Governor, and other key policymakers as we make Boston and its institutions more climate resilient.

From the 2016 Climate Ready Boston (CRB) research that comprehensively detailed the likely impacts of climate change on Boston, to the 2019 Carbon Free Boston (CFB) study that outlined the City's options for strategic electrification, to the 2023 Our Shared History report that encourages policymakers and developers to avoid, acknowledge, and address the racial mistakes of the past during a time of fundamental urban transformation, the GRC has set the table for cooperation and action (Boston Green Ribbon Commission, 2023a; City of Boston, 2016a). Along the way, it has helped shape and encourage participation in the ambitious agenda that puts Boston in the vanguard of the US cities addressing the challenges of climate change (City of Boston, 2022a).

THE CRITICAL ROLE OF HIGHER EDUCATION INSTITUTIONS

Mobilizing the higher education community has been a core strategy of the GRC from its inception. On a percentage basis, the Boston metro region has one of the densest concentrations of higher education of any city – ranking fourth nationally (Wakefield, 2021). Higher education organizations represent some of the City's largest landowners and energy users. They are responsible for a significant percentage of the City's emissions and many of them are directly in "harm's way" from future climate risks, especially coastal flooding.

Higher education institutions can play a unique role in informing, facilitating, and accelerating the urban climate transformation. Their research knowledge can inform investments and regulatory decision-making; their students can provide the critical skills needed by private and public stakeholders to support implementation; their campuses can act as "living labs" to test out innovative climate solutions; the creative power of faculty, staff, and students both graduate and undergraduate are unlike any other institution; and their political influence can help inform and advance needed public policy changes.

The GRC HEWG was launched in 2011 under the leadership of GRC member Katie Lapp, Executive Vice President of Harvard University, with a core membership of five higher education institutions that served on the GRC from its inception – Harvard, Boston University, MIT, Northeastern University, and University of Massachusetts, Boston. The working group was initially staffed by the Harvard Office for Sustainability with a small contract from the GRC. Over time, the participation in the working group expanded beyond the GRC members, and now also includes Emerson College, Tufts University, and Brandeis University.

In 2019, the staffing of the HEWG was transitioned to a third-party consultant, and the working group developed a five-year (2020–2025) strategic plan. The strategic plan is organized around the following core components:

- *Mission*: To leverage the higher education sector's capabilities for climate action by sharing knowledge and fostering collaboration within and across sectors for the City of Boston to meet its climate goals.
- *Vision*: The HEWG envisions a sustainable and resilient Boston where higher education institutions model sustainability, exemplify equitable climate mitigation and resilience, and support others in the transition to a more sustainable future.
- *Goals*: The working group is pursuing strategies to support four broad goals:

    1. Support climate action planning and implementation across the higher education sector.
    2. Facilitate collaborative research that leverages the higher education sector's capabilities to promote solutions for equitable climate resilience and mitigation in the greater Boston area.
    3. Transfer knowledge to other sectors to accelerate change for equitable implementation of climate mitigation and resilience.
    4. Develop the HEWG as a high-functioning collective of diverse institutions with cross-sectorial impact for the City's climate action plan implementation.

KEY CLIMATE ACTION CONTRIBUTIONS OF THE HEWG

Over the last decade, the HEWG has made critical contributions to the City of Boston's climate transformation.

Setting Aggressive Climate Goals and Action Plans

The members of the HEWG are aggressively reducing emissions by driving efficiency improvements in their buildings, reducing the energy intensity of laboratories, investing in large-scale renewable energy projects, leading research innovation, and testing cutting-edge solutions. In collaboration with local and state partners, their resiliency planning efforts are also helping to prepare and assist the region for the impacts of climate change to come, and the impacts already being felt. Table 6.1 shows some of the climate goals of the HEWG members.

Large Scale Renewable Energy Purchasing

The HEWG led the creation and launch of the GRC's Renewable Energy Purchasing Network beginning in 2015. The network supported GRC members in advancing the practice of making large-scale renewable energy purchases (10 MW or more) through Power Purchase Agreements (PPAs) or Virtual Power Purchase Agreements (VPPAs). At the time, the core challenges were institutional, and not market based. PPAs and VPPAs are complicated contractual arrangements that require dedicated energy management expertise. Most organizations lacked the internal capacity to manage these transactions.

Table 6.1. HEWG Climate Goals.

Boston University	Zero net emissions by 2030 for operations
Emerson College	Carbon neutrality by 2030
Harvard University	Fossil-fuel free by 2050 and fossil-fuel neutral by 2026
MIT	32% emissions reduction by 2030
Northeastern University	80% reduction in emissions per square foot by 2050
Tufts University	Carbon neutrality by 2050
University of Massachusetts, Boston	Carbon neutrality by 2050

Over its five-year existence, the network spawned multiple innovations, including:

- A series of knowledge products[5] to help large organizations manage renewable energy procurement:
  - A guide to institutional renewable energy procurement.
  - A guide to making valid renewable energy impact claims.
  - Guidance on structuring PPA and VPPA purchasing contracts.
- Creation of the renewable energy purchasing prize.
- Execution of the largest multi-owner PPA agreement in the country – 60 MW of solar power with three separate off-takers.

As a result of the network capacity building, large-scale RE procurement has now become a much more standard business practice for large Boston-based energy users.

Consensus Climate Impact Forecast

HEWG institutions provided the scientific leadership to establish a consensus forecast for future Boston climate impacts – sea level rise, extreme precipitation, coastal storms, and extreme heat. This forecast was in turn used by the City to shape its resilience planning and regulatory regime.

As part of the City's CRB resilience plan (which was strategically supported by the GRC), the University of Massachusetts, Boston took the lead in organizing the Boston Research Advisory Group (BRAG), which brought together world class climate scientists from 10 universities (University of Massachusetts – Boston, Boston University, Harvard, Tufts, Rutgers, MIT, University of Massachusetts – Lowell, University of Massachusetts – Amherst, Cornell, and Northeastern) to develop a consensus on what level of climate disruptions the City should plan on addressing in its citywide resilience strategies (Boston Research Advisory Group, 2016).

As a result of the BRAG 2015 report, the Boston Planning and Development Agency (BPDA), which controls permitting for all large new construction and renovations in the City, implemented requirements that all new developments demonstrate resilience to a minimum of 40" of sea level rise.[6] BRAG projections have also been integrated into the stormwater management plans for the Boston Water and Sewer Commission, as well as the City's Extreme Heat Resilience plan.

The consensus forecast is updated every five years, with the most recent update occurring in 2022. In early 2024, Massachusetts Governor Maura Healey announced her intention to create a state-level Office of Climate Science that will apply the BRAG methodology to create a state-level consensus climate forecast (Commonwealth of Massachusetts, 2024b).

City Decarbonization Pathways Analysis

In 2017, the City of Boston formally asked the GRC to establish a CFB working group to provide recommendations to the City on decarbonization pathways to achieve its goal of being carbon neutral by 2050. The working group provided design input and fundraising support for the CFB report. The GRC partnered with the Institute for Sustainable Energy (now the Institute for Global Sustainability) at Boston University to design and develop the CFB report. Additional HEWG members – MIT and Northeastern – provided critical consulting support.

The CFB process brought together a broad set of stakeholders with an interest in, and knowledge to contribute to, Boston's clean energy future. The CFB report analyzed detailed strategies to guide Boston's transition to a renewable-energy future (Boston Green Ribbon Commission, 2019). In addition to a summary report, the CFB project developed six supplemental reports on social equity, energy, buildings, transportation, waste, and carbon offsets.

The reports helped to shape the City's strategy to achieve carbon neutrality by 2050, which will require dramatic changes in city energy systems, including large improvements in building energy efficiency, decarbonization of the electricity grid, and the electrification of transportation and building heating and cooling. The City's decarbonization strategies in the 2019 Climate Action Plan update were largely based on the analysis in the CFB report (City of Boston, 2019).

Resilience Governance and Finance

HEWG member, University of Massachusetts, Boston, provided research and best practice reports on three key climate resilience issues.

- A report on options for resilience governance structures, including a structure for resilience authorities at the neighborhood, municipal, or regional scale (Kruel et al., 2018).
- A report on options for financing the $6–$8 billion in resilience investments that will be required to protect the City from sea level rise and coastal flooding (Sustainable Solutions Lab, 2018a).
- A report analyzing the feasibility of a harbor-wide barrier system as an alternative to shoreline protections (Sustainable Solutions Lab, 2018b). This report concluded that a harbor barrier would not effectively protect the city from sea level rise and would not be cost effective.

Best Practice Sharing

The HEWG has played a central role in facilitating best practice sharing among higher education institutions, and between the higher education sector and other Boston sectors. Examples include the following:

- *Lab benchmarking*: Higher education is a major user of lab space in the city, which can use up to ten times the energy and four times the water of an average building. The HEWG partnered with Eversource, the Boston electricity utility, and Lab21 to host a series of forums on best practices in lab energy efficiency. This included the publishing of two lab energy use benchmarking reports. The reports developed a new lab building benchmarking dataset comprised of 121 Boston-area higher-education labs, with data quality exceeding that of any other sample.

- *Next generation climate action planning.* Many higher education institutions have been leaders in the climate action planning field. The HEWG has held multiple best practice sharing events to advance the adoption of leading practices.

- *Climate justice and health intersections.* The HEWG sponsored a series of three webinars sharing expertise from researchers and environmental justice practitioners exploring how systemic racism and intentional environmental pollution have caused poor health in vulnerable communities across Boston and how we can use climate investments to reverse these harms, including how retrofitting of low-income households can produce the co-benefits of cleaner air, reduced health risks, lower energy costs, and reduced emissions.

- *Climate innovation tours.* Two GRC climate innovation tours focused on recent higher education projects, including: (1) a collaborative research project between GreenRoots and the Boston University School of Public Health; and (2) the Boston University Center for Computing and Data Science, a 340,000 SF building fully heated and cooled by 31 1,500 foot geothermal wells, making it the largest geothermal building in Boston.

- *Collaborative climate action planning.* Multiple higher education institutions have participated in the GRC's Collaborative Climate Action Planning initiative, which is a 12-month program that takes a cohort of 6–8 organizations through the process of creating a climate action plan that addresses emissions reductions, climate resilience, and climate justice.

- *Organizational climate justice.* In 2023, the GRC is launching a learning network of GRC members and working group participants to advance best practices in organizational climate justice strategies. An organizational climate justice strategy identifies and implements specific opportunities for the organization to use its climate action plan (carbon mitigation and resiliency) to improve the health and wellbeing of its stakeholders and the communities it is located in. HEWG members have been leaders in this effort.

Influencing Key Policy Decisions

Members of the HEWG have provided detailed input and feedback to help shape key City and state climate policies. In many cases, this has involved helping the City understand how climate policies affect campus operations as opposed to individual buildings and how those policies can be better structured to support campus scale energy and resilience goals. These policies include the following:

- The Boston Building Emissions Reduction and Disclosure Ordinance (BERDO), which mandates that buildings above 20,000 square feet reduce their emissions to meet prescribed five-year reductions that achieve carbon neutrality by 2050 (City of Boston, 2018).

- The Boston Zero Net Carbon Zoning Overlay District (ZNC Zoning) will require all large new developments to achieve carbon neutrality on the date of occupancy (City of Boston, 2024).

- The Municipal Opt-In Specialized Stretch Energy Code, is a state-level building code to advance building carbon neutrality (Commonwealth of Massachusetts, 2022).

- The Three-Year Energy Efficiency Plans direct the spending of over $3 billion in ratepayer funds for energy efficiency incentives (Commonwealth of Massachusetts, 2024a). The GRC has been a leader in providing input into these plans from the commercial and industrial sector point of view.

SOME LESSONS LEARNED

The decade-plus experience of the GRC and its HEWG has advanced some important lessons about how higher education can play a leadership role in the next generation of urban climate transformation.

- *Collaboration increases impact*: It is difficult for individual institutions to have a significant impact on the design of the cities they are located in. But when institutions collaborate within and across sectors, the impact can be transformational.

- *It takes time to build trust*: Both the GRC and the HEWG have had remarkable stability in their participation. The same five institutions that were part of the founding of the GRC in 2010 are still actively engaged. In many cases, leadership has changed but organizational commitments have stayed steady. And in many other cases, the same individuals have been engaged for over a decade. This has allowed the building of personal trust within social networks, which is a key institutional asset for making change.

- *A neutral convening table is enormously useful*: Both the GRC and the HEWG have been able to advance issues because they represent a safe place for multiple stakeholders to have strategic engagements, they would otherwise be reluctant to engage in. This effect was a key success ingredient in both CRB and CFB. And in both initiatives, the credibility of the academic leaders was key to getting stakeholders to accept the results. There was never any serious political objection to either the climate impact forecasts or the decarbonization pathways analysis because they were produced by highly credible research organizations.

- *Civic leadership can facilitate political continuity*: One of the reasons the GRC was created was to provide some continuity during political transitions. During the last 12 years, Boston has had three governors and four mayors (Wikipedia, 2024).

In every transition, the GRC met with the newly elected leaders after their victories and emphasized the need to continue the work that had begun under earlier administrations. Because of the stature of the GRC members, this helped avoid the typical instincts of new political leaders to throw out what had been done before them and start over. As a result, there has been remarkably steady progress on climate action over multiple leadership regimes.

FUTURE DIRECTIONS

The City of Boston has entered a critical new phase in its climate work – shifting from analysis and planning to implementation – from a focus on the "what" (what strategies do we need to implement for long-term resilience and carbon neutrality?) to a focus on the "how" (how do we implement these strategies so that they achieve scale within the necessary time frame, are affordable, lead to equitable outcomes, and improve the quality of life in the city?) All stakeholders need to pivot quickly to making change happen "on the ground" and start working out the very practical details of what resilience and carbon neutrality look like across multiple sectors and at multiple scales. While significant progress has been made, there continues to be a huge gap between the city's resilience and emissions reduction aspirations and the governance and finance capacity needed to make those aspirations real. Cities around the United States, especially those with a large volume of higher education institutions, can create a network of shared innovations and ideas similar to the HEWG. Now more than ever, it is crucial to use what shared resources we have to build a more resilient future.

With its broad base of stakeholders, the GRC will play an important role in advancing the "state of the art" in climate action implementation and building the political will to take on the "heavy lifts" needed to achieve success. Higher education institutions will continue to be key players in this work, leveraging their best practices, research capacity, student activism, and policy influence to make climate action happen at a transformative scale. Some of the opportunities for future action and influence include the following:

- More fully leveraging the "Campus as Lab" opportunities to have universities play the role of "applied R&D labs" at the edge of climate innovation.
- Strengthen the anchor institution strategies of higher education institutions to use their organizational assets to advance climate justice in the communities they are located in.
- Advance the role of higher education in solving the talent gaps in climate-critical occupations.
- Solve the dilemma of how to decarbonize large district energy systems and CHP plants that are dependent on natural gas.

2030, 2040, or even 2050 may sound like they are a long way away, but in the timeline of structural urban change, they are right around the corner. Over this time, we will need to eliminate the use of natural gas and other fossil fuels, decarbonize 100% of our electricity, electrify our homes and our transportation, eliminate all waste, build coastal protection infrastructure on our 47 miles of shoreline, implement massive green infrastructure to protect from flooding and prepare for extreme heat. The good news is that we do know how to do almost all of these things. The caution is that we have not yet achieved the political will to implement them at scale and on the timeline needed. The leadership of higher education institutions in Boston will be critical to make this happen.

NOTES

1. Since 2009, the Barr Foundations climate funding has increased from $10 million a year to now over $50 million a year.

2. Based on authors' direct knowledge of discussions.

3. In this context, the term "Commission" can be misleading. The GRC is totally independent of city government and does not even have its own

legal structure, instead operating under the fiscal sponsorship of a local non-profit.

4. Based on authors' knowledge of GRC operations.

5. All of these reports can be found on the GRC website at www.greenribboncommission.org.

6. Authors' discussions with BPDA staff responsible for resilience standards in the permitting process.

REFERENCES

Boston Green Ribbon Commission. (2019). *Carbon free Boston: Summary report.* https://greenribboncommission.org/document/executive-summary-carbon-free-boston-2/

Boston Green Ribbon Commission. (2023a). *About.* https://greenribboncommission.org/about/

Boston Green Ribbon Commission. (2023b, March). *Our shared history – Using Boston's climate opportunities to address systemic racism.* https://greenribboncommission.org/document/boston-green-ribbon-commission-and-embrace-boston-our-shared-history-report/

Boston Research Advisory Group. (2016, June 1). *Climate change and sea level rise projections for Boston.* https://www.boston.gov/sites/default/files/file/document_files/2016/12/brag_report_-_final.pdf

City of Boston. (2010) *Sparking Boston's climate revolution.* https://www.cityofboston.gov/images_documents/bca_full_rprt_r5_tcm3-19558.pdf

City of Boston. (2016a, December). *Climate Ready Boston executive summary.* https://www.boston.gov/sites/default/files/file/2023/03/2016_climate_ready_boston_executive_summary_1.pdf

City of Boston. (2016b). *Imagine Boston 2030.* https://www.boston.gov/sites/default/files/embed/i/imagine-boston-executive_summary.pdf

City of Boston. (2018, March 28). *Building emissions reduction and disclosure.* https://www.boston.gov/departments/environment/building-emissions-reduction-and-disclosure

City of Boston. (2019, October). *2019 climate action plan update.* https://www.boston.gov/sites/default/files/embed/file/2019-10/city_of_boston_2019_climate_action_plan_update_4.pdf

City of Boston. (2022a, October). Boston climate action. https://www.boston.gov/departments/environment/boston-climate-action

City of Boston. (2022b). *Audit of city-owned land completed.* https://www.boston.gov/news/audit-city-owned-land-completed#:~:text=The%20City%20and%20its%20municipal,promise%20of%20transformative%20community%20development.

City of Boston. (2024) *2024 Net zero carbon zoning initiative.* https://www.bostonplans.org/zoning/zoning-initiatives/2024-net-zero-carbon-zoning-initiative

Commonwealth of Massachusetts. (2022). *Final code language for stretch code update and new specialized stretch code.* https://www.mass.gov/info-details/stretch-energy-code-development-2022#final-code-language-for-stretch-code-update-and-new-specialized-stretch-code-

Commonwealth of Massachusetts. (2024a). *EEAC energy efficiency three-year planning.* https://www.mass.gov/info-details/eeac-energy-efficiency-three-year-planning

Commonwealth of Massachusetts. (2024b, January 1). *Healy–Driscoll administration launches climate science advisory council.* https://www.mass.gov/orgs/office-of-climate-science-ocs

Kruel, S., Herst, R., & Cash, D. (2018). *Governance for a changing climate: Adapting Boston's built environment for increased flooding.* School for the Environment Publications. 6. https://scholarworks.umb.edu/cgi/viewcontent.cgi?article=1005&context=environment_pubs

Milando, C. W., Black-Ingersoll, F., Heidari, L., López-Hernández, I., de Lange, J., Negassa, A., Mcintyre, A., Martinez, M., Bongiovanni, R., Levy, J., Kinney, P., Scammell, M., & Fabian, M. P. (2022). Mixed methods assessment of personal heat exposure, sleep, physical activity, and heat adaptation strategies among urban residents in the Boston area, MA. *BMC Public Health*, 22(1), 1–11.

Rantz, R. (2002). Leading urban institutions of higher education in the new millennium. *Leadership & Organization Development Journal*, 23(8), 456–466.

Sustainable Solutions Lab, U Mass Boston. (2018a, April 4). *Financing climate resilience*. https://greenribboncommission.org/document/financing-climate-resilience-report/

Sustainable Solutions Lab, U Mass Boston. (2018b, May 4). *Feasibility of harbor wide barrier systems*. https://greenribboncommission.org/document/executive-summary-feasibility-of-harbor-wide-barrier-systems-preliminary-analysis-for-boston-harbor/

Thorns, D. C. (2017). *The transformation of cities: Urban theory and urban life*. Bloomsbury Publishing.

Wakefield, R. (2021, July 29). *The cities with the most colleges and universities in the USA*. https://www.aspireatlantic.com/post/the-cities-with-the-most-colleges-universities-in-the-usa

Wikipedia. (2024). Governor of Massachusetts. https://en.wikipedia.org/wiki/Governor_of_Massachusetts; Mayor of Boston. https://en.wikipedia.org/wiki/Mayor_of_Boston

7

BUILDING A CITY–UNIVERSITY PARTNERSHIP FOR ACCELERATING URBAN CLIMATE NEUTRALITY: THE CASE OF VALÈNCIA (SPAIN)

Jordi Peris Blanes[a], Oksana Udovyk[a], Fermín Cerezo[b], Guillermo Palau[a], Iván Cuesta[c], Dionisio Ortiz Miranda[d], Jose Luis Alaponte[e], Débora Domingo[e], Carla Montagud[f], Ana Escario Chust[a], Sergio Segura Calero[a] and Pablo Aranguiz Mesias[a]

[a]*INGENIO [CSIC-UPV], Universitat Politècnica de València, Spain*
[b]*València City Council, Spain*
[c]*Institute for Energy Engineering, Universitat Politècnica de València, Spain*
[d]*Group of International Economy and Development, Department of Economics and Social Sciences, Universitat Politècnica de València, Spain*
[e]*Architectural Projects Department, Universitat Politècnica de València, Spain*
[f]*School of Industrial Engineering, Universitat Politècnica de València, Spain*

ABSTRACT

City–university partnerships (CUPs) are emerging as dynamic collaborations addressing urban challenges in various cities. This chapter delves into the transformative dynamics of the CUP in

Valencia, particularly within the framework of the European Union (EU) Cities Mission. Valencia, a recognized leader, achieved the EU Mission Label in 2023, showcasing the success of its collaboration with the Polytechnic University of València (UPV). The Valencian CUP functions as a multi-faceted entity, serving as a knowledge powerhouse, an innovation catalyst in urban policies, and a vital educational space. The exploration unfolds various dimensions of the CUP's impact, emphasizing its contributions to the city's development model, innovation in urban policies, and transdisciplinary education. Examining collaborations and transformations leading to CUP creation and effective functioning through the multi-level perspective (MLP) framework illuminates a complexity of the CUP in Valencia. It also highlights the catalytic role of the EU Cities Mission in shaping CUP creation. In conclusion, the CUP in Valencia stands as a beacon of inspiration and a blueprint for global urban centers navigating the path toward climate neutrality. This chapter contributes valuable insights to the broader discourse on the transformative potential of CUPs, acknowledging the narrative as ongoing and calling for further research to uncover their full potential in shaping resilient and sustainable urban landscapes.

Keywords: City–university partnerships; city transformation; multi-stakeholder collaboration; mission-oriented academia; climate-neutral cities; transformative universities

1. INTRODUCTION

CUPs have emerged as dynamic collaborations between city and academic institutions, serving as crucibles for innovative solutions to pressing urban challenges (Caughman et al., 2023; Keeler et al., 2019, 2023). These partnerships leverage the unique strengths of cities and universities to foster sustainable development, resilience, and transformative change (Caughman et al., 2020), seeking to blend the intellectual power of academic research with the practical insights and needs of urban governance (Allen et al., 2017; AtKisson, 2012).

Within this context, our exploration delves into the intricacies of CUPs, casting a spotlight on their role in advancing the EU's ambitious mission to achieve over 100 climate-neutral and smart cities by 2030 through its "Cities Mission." This initiative aims to engage local authorities and stakeholders in delivering climate-neutral and smart cities, which will act as hubs for experimentation and innovation to enable all European cities to transition to climate neutrality by 2050 (EC, 2021).

To delve into greater detail, our attention will be centered on the CUP dynamics in the city of Valencia, Spain. This vibrant metropolis is one of the carefully chosen 100 cities participating in the EU Cities Mission. Nestled amidst an industrial metropolitan area and an orchard acknowledged as an agricultural world heritage site, Valencia stands out with its predominantly service-oriented economy. Recognized as the World Design Capital in 2022 (World Design Organization, 2019) and a frontrunner city in the European Capital of Innovation Award in 2020 and 2022, it has also been awarded the Green European Capital 2024 title for its sustainability policies.

In a landmark achievement in 2023, Valencia proudly secured the EU Mission Label, a recognition given by the EU to the cities that have successfully developed plans for their climate neutrality (European Commission, 2023). This label is a significant achievement and sets an example for other cities to follow in the transition to a climate-neutral future (Ayuntamiento de València, 2023a). This notable accolade positions Valencia at the forefront of European cities actively aligning with the EU's overarching mission to realize Net-Zero Cities, notably propelled by the strategic CUP established to fulfill this ambitious climate mission.

The collaboration between Valencia and the Universitat Politècnica de València (UPV) (known locally in Valencia as the "binomial university–city") emerges as an exemplary case study within the broader framework of CUPs. Purposefully aligned with the EU's mission of Net-Zero Cities, this partnership serves as a microcosm reflecting the broader European endeavor to combat climate change (Dóci et al., 2022; Soberón et al., 2023) and wider field of urban sustainability transformation studies (Keeler et al., 2023). As cities worldwide grapple with the complexities of urban sustainability transformation and climate change mission, Valencia's collaboration with UPV stands as an example of the power of inter-institutional partnerships in steering cities toward a more sustainable and resilient future. Our analysis traverses the various initiatives, governance frameworks, and collaborative mechanisms that define this strategic partnership.

That way, our chapter embarks on a comprehensive journey into the realm of CUP, focusing specifically on the dynamic collaboration between Valencia and UPV in the context of the EU's mission for Net-Zero Cities. As the imperative for sustainable urban development becomes increasingly paramount, the insights gleaned from this case study illuminate the transformative potential of CUPs within the broader mission-oriented policies of the EU.

2. THE CUP FOR ACCELERATING CLIMATE NEUTRALITY IN VALÈNCIA

Our exploration of the CUP in Valencia commences with the València 2030 Urban Strategy (Ayuntamiento de València, 2023b), a cornerstone of the future València 2030 Climate Mission (Ayuntamiento de València, 2023a). Adopted in 2020, this strategy serves as a collaborative framework guiding the city's long-term transformation process, laying out a roadmap for a diversity of city institutions and actors across different scales.

It rests on three fundamental characteristics, making it a robust and influential strategy. First, the València 2030 Urban Strategy aligns itself with the well-established and legitimate goals outlined by the UN Urban Agenda (UN-Habitat, 2016). Second, it recognizes the complexities of contemporary urban challenges, endorsing a learning-oriented approach, as articulated by Bulkeley (2016). This perspective emphasizes the cycle of innovating, experimenting, testing, encountering failures, and learning from them as a catalyst for accelerating urban sustainability transitions. Third, the strategy acknowledges the imperative for additional resources and is aligned with the priorities outlined in various European programs, such as the EU Next Generation Funds (EC, 2023).

However, the pivotal aspect of the València 2030 Urban Strategy is the mission-oriented innovation approach (Mazzucato, 2018) that takes center stage for the first time. This approach seamlessly integrates into the core of the urban strategy, acting as a complementary force within the innovation realm to enhance key urban policies derived from the Urban Agenda.

Consequently, the city of València enthusiastically embraced the "100 climate-neutral and smart cities for 2030" EU Mission, aiming to facilitate city transformations, accelerate the implementation of the Paris Agreement, and act as a catalyst for realizing the European Green Pact (EC, 2021). This marks a significant leap toward a sustainable and climate-neutral future for València, intertwining global goals with local strategies.

Valencia's commitment to sustainability has recently garnered recognition, as it attained the status of a Mission City for the quality of its Climate City Contract, presented to the European Commission within the European Cities Mission (Ayuntamiento de València, 2023a). Valencia stands among the first 10 cities to receive this prestigious award.

This success is underpinned by a distinct rationale characterized by several key features:

- *Combination of the Urban Agenda and the Climate Mission*: Valencia strategically integrates the Urban Agenda and the Climate Mission, synergistically propelling the city's urban transition toward sustainability and climate neutrality.
- *Goal orientation*: The mission's approach is firmly rooted in a pragmatic yet ambitious goal of attaining climate neutrality by 2030, aligning with the EU mission's objectives.
- *Political consensus*: The initiative secures a broad political consensus, ensuring the sustained momentum of initiatives beyond electoral cycles.
- *Crosscutting and silo-breaking orientation*: Embracing a fully crosscutting approach, the initiative breaks down silos within organizations, institutions, and knowledge domains, fostering a holistic and integrated perspective.
- *Multi-actor and MLP*: The approach mobilizes diverse stakeholders into a city alliance for climate neutrality, adopting a distributed leadership model to ensure widespread involvement.
- *Strong CUP creation*: A robust university–city binomial is established, forming a strategic collaboration to address complex challenges and integrate science, research, and innovation into the city's transformation process.

Through the final point, creation of the CUP, the city aimed to strategically and transversally incorporate the vectors of science, research, and innovation into the city's transformation process. CUP establishes a space for co-governance, dialogue, and collaboration between the university and the city, offering mutual benefits in several dimensions.

To steer and propel the development of the CUP, a formal agreement was officially defined and signed. This agreement structures the strategic lines of collaboration and establishes a governance structure as illustrated in Fig. 7.1. This structured governance approach ensures effective coordination and execution of initiatives within the CUP.

The governance structure of the Valencia CUP is a well-orchestrated framework designed to facilitate collaboration, innovation, and strategic decision-making. It revolves around a Strategic Commission, chaired by the City Mayor and the University Chancellor, to define the key objectives and priorities for research and action.

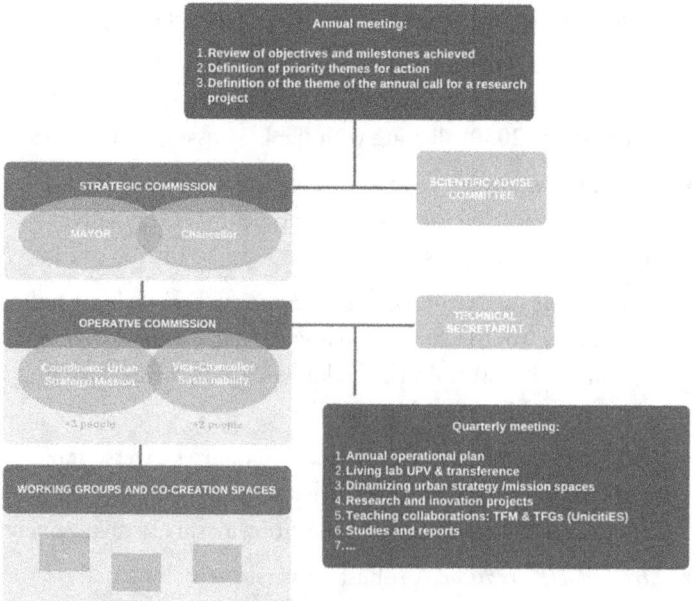

Fig. 7.1. Governance Structure for the Valencia CUP.
Source: The authors.

It is advised by a Scientific Committee made up of renowned scientists. The Head of the Operative Commission is shared by the Vice-Chancellor for Sustainability on the side of the University and the Coordinator of Urban Strategies on the side of the City Council. Their work is complemented by up to three key members, who define the Annual Operative Plan and all the tasks related to the UPV Living Lab, the dynamization of urban strategy or mission spaces, the deployment of research and innovation projects, the teaching collaborations and the elaboration of specific studies and reports. This dual leadership ensures a cohesive approach that blends day-to-day operations with long-term vision. The engagement is further enriched by working groups and co-creation spaces, fostering collaboration between city and university representatives.

This comprehensive structure facilitates the dynamism of the CUP, integrating research, innovation projects, educational collaborations, and the Living Lab UPV's initiatives, all under the umbrella of a shared commitment to sustainable urban development and the EU climate (EC, 2021).

3. A MULTI-LEVEL FRAMEWORK TO UNDERSTAND UNIVERSITY TRANSFORMATION

In order to comprehend the transformative dynamics within the university that have given rise to the CUP, we leverage the MLP (Geels, 2002; Geels & Schot, 2007; Smith et al., 2010) as a robust theory of change for socio-technical transitions. This perspective posits that transition processes evolve through the intricate interplay of three analytical levels: the regime, niches, and the landscape.

The regime signifies the established order in a socio-technical system, such as energy production, consumption, mobility, and, in this context, higher education. Niches represent spaces where innovators experiment with alternatives, akin to initiatives in renewable energy and alternative production cooperatives. Meanwhile, the landscape, influenced by factors like resource scarcity and climate change, has the potential to destabilize the regime, opening opportunities for niche innovations. This interplay between the three levels is a common thread connecting them all.

Universities, when examined through this socio-technical lens, reveal similar interactions and challenges observed in broader contexts like cities or neighborhoods (Leal & Bardi, 2019). Campuses can be considered living labs and experimental spaces, serving as testing grounds for technological and social solutions in decarbonization, which can later be applied to urban environments (Kumdokrub et al., 2023; Tian et al., 2022).

Taking the case of UPV into account, the MLP reveals distinct trends and initiatives across the three analytical levels. At the *landscape level*, and within the timeframe of Fig. 7.2, the UPV became progressively aligned with global warming concerns and climate emergency, incorporating the Sustainable Development Goals into research and education. Given this background, the UPV embraced the EU Climate Mission by committing to become a carbon-neutral campus by 2030 as part of the 100 Climate-Neutral and Smart Cities Mission (see Section 2 for more details). At *regime level*, two

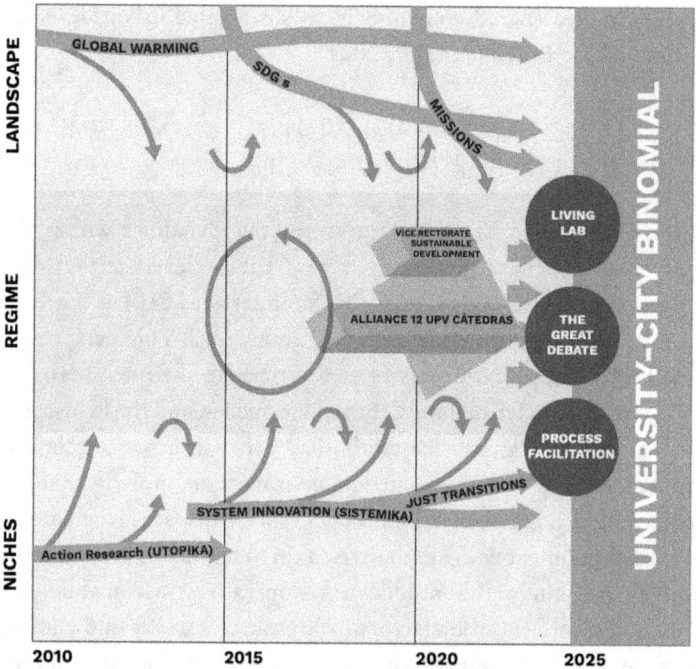

Fig. 7.2. An MLP of the Key University Transformation Processes.
Source: The authors.

pivotal changes emerged for the building of the city–university binomial. On one hand, the emergence of a sustainability alliance with 12 chairs devoted to different key urban issues such as energy or agri-food that promoted the Great Debate (see Section 4 – The Alliance of UPV Chairs for Sustainability), and on the other, the mission-oriented approach taken by the Vice-Rectorate of Sustainable Development in 2020 and its Living Labs initiatives (see Sections 5 and 6). At *niche level*, several initiatives took place at the university that created the conditions for the emergence of the binomial. On the one hand, some pedagogical initiatives that started as an action-learning approach that evolved into just transition activities aimed to reshape the university's educational model (see Section 8 – Education for a Just Transitions). On the other hand, the involvement in action research and multi-actors' participation, such as the Energy Transition Multi-stakeholder Board, enabled new ways of interaction between university and city actors leading to new forms of facilitating urban processes (see Section 7). All these multi-level elements form the enabling conditions for the emergence of the CUP in València.

4. THE ALLIANCE OF UPV CHAIRS FOR SUSTAINABILITY

Expanding upon the foundational dynamics within the university detailed in the preceding section, we now turn our attention to the trends and initiatives unfolding at the regime level. At this juncture of our exploration, a pivotal facet of the CUP comes to the fore with the establishment of the Alliance of UPV Chairs for Sustainability within the university.

In the year 2020, 12 distinct chairs (commonly referred to as "cátedras" in Spanish, denoting specialized professorships) financed either by the city or the regional government, spanning diverse domains, including energy transition, climate change, and climate governance, coalesced under the umbrella of the sustainability to form the alliance. Serving as vital knowledge hubs, these chairs play a pivotal role in generating and disseminating information crucial to the realization of Valencia's urban transformation (Holmberg et al., 2012).

The alliance brings together research groups, students, and policymakers, fostering research, providing cutting-edge sustainability education, and co-innovating public policies. One tangible contribution is the creation of spaces for knowledge exchange between UPV and the city, specifically addressing matters related to the climate mission.

Since 2020, the alliance has orchestrated four annual conferences, each serving as a milestone in the ongoing collaboration. The inaugural event in October 2020, the hackathon "Decarbonize the Vera Campus," set the tone for subsequent engagements. In October 2021, the conference "The UPV Responds to the Mission for a Neutral City Valencia" provided a crucial platform for discussions on the cooperation between the university and the city. Notably, during this conference, the Rector of the UPV announced the institution's commitment to achieving carbon neutrality by 2030 (UPV, 2022b). Additionally, the event hosted a co-design workshop for the UPV Living Lab, laying the groundwork for its subsequent implementation.

The momentum continued with the "The UPV–City Alliance for the València 2030 Climate Mission" conference in October 2022 and culminated in the October 2023 conference, "The UPV in the Mission of Climate-Neutral Cities," co-hosted by the Chair of Urban Energy Transition and the Vice-Rectorate for Sustainable Development of the Campuses. These annual gatherings complement a rich array of conferences, workshops, training sessions, and informative events organized by the 12 chairs of the alliance.

Beyond conferences, the alliance is proactive in exploring how the university should transform to transition toward carbon neutrality. Two interrelated activities have been undertaken for this purpose. First, envisioning the university under different carbon-neutral scenarios was carried out through a foresight workshop involving professors, researchers, staff, and students. The resulting alternative scenarios illuminate the diverse impacts on campus structure, teaching methods, and governance. Second, the Grand Debate, a survey involving 2,228 responses from the UPV community, gauged views on specific policies and initiatives for carbon-neutral campuses (UPV, 2022a). This survey not only provided valuable insights into the degree of commitment to climate action within the university community but also identified paths of both greatest and least resistance to change. The findings could be of use for urban strategic planning in Valencia (Guerrieri et al., 2019).

In summary, the alliance of 12 UPV chairs emerges as a central player in the CUP, making pivotal contributions. First, these chairs generate and transfer knowledge crucial to the development of València 2030 Climate Mission. Second, the alliance serves as a dynamic space for mutual learning, shaping urban policies through experiments and innovations. Third, the chairs actively assist the Vice-Rectorate of Sustainable Development of UPV Campuses in formulating policies for a sustainable campus transformation. Lastly, by leveraging the legitimacy of the UPV, the alliance facilitates broader processes of dialogue, governance, and co-design of urban policies for the climate mission.

5. THE VICE-RECTORATE OF SUSTAINABLE DEVELOPMENT AND THE LIVING LAB EXPERIENCE

Building upon the transformative developments at the regime level discussed in Section 3, we now turn our attention to the Vice-Rectorate of Sustainable Development, which is responsible for the planning and execution of the infrastructures as well as the maintenance, improvement, and adaptation to saving and sustainability policies of its equipment, buildings, and facilities. It is also responsible for the coordination and execution of the institution's environmental policies and the ecological transition of the university campuses. After the Alliance of UPV Chair Conference, this Vice-Rectorate assumes the mandate to lead the mission on university campuses' climate neutrality. This move exemplifies the ongoing changes in the socio-technical system (as elaborated in Section 3) and further solidifies the university's dedication to carbon neutrality by 2030 (UPV, 2023d).

The Vice-Rectorate's commitment to the net-zero mission paved the way for the inception of the UPV Living Lab, a groundbreaking test bed and experimentation environment unveiled in October 2022 (UPV, 2023b). Functioning as a dynamic arena for co-creation, exploration, and experimentation, the Living Lab facilitates collaborative efforts among the university community, users, and producers. Guided by open innovation principles, it employs iterative processes focused on sustainable impact, acting as a crucial intermediary between citizens, academia, business, and public administration.

The UPV Living Lab, situated on the main campus, serves as an on-campus laboratory designed to expedite the journey toward carbon neutrality for both the UPV and the city of Valencia. This innovative space allows for the implementation of diverse projects and test benches, creating a sandbox of ideas replicable in Valencia's neighborhoods. It is considered a seed for the development of strategic projects in innovation and research, fostering collaboration between the university and the city.

In October 2022, the Vice-Rectorate for Sustainable Development of Campus initiated the first call for UPV Living Lab projects. This call aimed to inspire and facilitate innovative projects within the campus, seeking proposals aligned with the objectives of the climate mission and the decarbonization of UPV campuses. Proposals were encouraged to cover the entire project lifecycle, from design and development to testing and evaluation within the UPV campus environment.

The Vice-Rectorate office is committed to ensuring the availability and use of spaces and facilities, providing necessary support, monitoring and assessing results, and enhancing project visibility through UPV communication channels. Proposals, accepted at any Technology Readiness Level, underwent a thorough evaluation process.

Seven projects were selected in the first phase based on twelve received dossiers. Covering diverse topics, these projects involve participants from the entire university community, including professors, researchers, administrative staff, and students. As of now, four projects are actively being monitored in various implementation phases:

- The "Living Lab ETSII Project," initiated by the School of Industrial Engineers, is a focused endeavor aimed at visualizing energy transition actions within one building (5N) on the campus. This project serves as a dynamic platform to showcase and monitor the implementation of energy transition measures, providing an authentic learning environment for students and highlighting sustainable practices in the built environment.

- The "Eco-efficient Scientific Hosting Laboratory" seeks to monitor life within a housing prototype, gathering key indicators on space and energy consumption. This project is dedicated to developing and implementing sustainable practices in the design and operation of scientific laboratories, with a particular emphasis on enhancing energy efficiency and conserving resources.

- The pilot project, "Implementing Sustainable Urban Drainage Systems (SUDS) to Catalyze the Transformation Toward a More Resilient, Biodiverse, and Climate-neutral University Campus," focuses on optimal water resource management. Its goal is to seamlessly integrate sustainable urban drainage systems into the university campus, mitigating the impact of stormwater runoff, fostering biodiversity, and promoting climate resilience.

- Lastly, "The 4th Leaves No Trace" is a community decarbonization initiative concentrated on the fourth floor of the Nexus administrative building. This project emphasizes resource sharing and encourages low-impact daily routines as part of a broader initiative to engage administrative staff and occupants in adopting sustainable practices. Its aim is to reduce energy consumption and minimize environmental impact through behavior change and resource optimization.

In summary, the mission-oriented focus of the Vice-Rectorate of Sustainable Development and the subsequent launch of the UPV Living Lab signify paramount regime-level changes, affirming the university's proactive stance toward achieving carbon neutrality and fostering collaborative innovation within the UPV and city community and beyond.

6. THE ETSII MISSION INITIATIVE

Building on the commitment to carbon neutrality articulated by the university during the Alliance of UPV Chair Conferences (see Section 3), the School of Industrial Engineering (ETSII) has assumed a pivotal role in spearheading the collaborative efforts between the university and the city toward climate neutrality (Ayuntamiento de València, 2023a). With a substantial community comprising 4,000 students and 350 professors, ETSII aspires not only to exemplify sustainable practices within its domain but also to serve as a model to emulate both within and beyond its boundaries. This commitment is underscored by the inclusion of sustainability as a top priority in the ETSII2025 Strategic Plan from 2021 to 2025.

The Climate-Neutral ETSII Project, initiated in May 2022 and scheduled to conclude in December 2025, is a comprehensive initiative embodying ETSII's dedication to sustainability. It is not only one of the four UPV Living Lab projects but also a global initiative in itself. To ensure a multi-disciplinary approach, a diverse team was formed, including professors specialized in various engineering domains, UPV environmental unit representatives, students contributing to their final theses, and specialized companies. In pursuit of replicability, the collaboration extended to CATENERG, the chair of Energy Transition in Cities at UPV (UPV, 2023c).

The project is structured around six working packages, each playing a distinct role in achieving sustainability goals. The first one is dedicated to the coordination of the whole initiative. The second focuses on accurately measuring ETSII's carbon footprint and proposing effective actions to reduce it. The third one aims to establish living labs within the school to promote best practices in fighting climate change. The fourth explores key areas of intervention such as reducing, reusing, recycling, or renaturalising. The fifth proposes a pilot project for more sustainable mobility on the UPV campus. The sixth aims to involve the ETSII community, fostering a sense of belonging and empowering individuals in the decarbonization process.

The project's first phase introduced the LivingLAB-ETSII pilot project, to be unfolded between 2023 and 2024. It is a pilot project under the UPV Living Lab scheme initiated by the Vice-Rector's Office for Sustainable Campus. This pilot aims to elevate ETSII's sustainability by establishing a benchmark for climate change mitigation practices and raising awareness among 80% of ETSII's community regarding the carbon footprint of their activities. Situated in the ETSII 5N building, dedicated to lectures, this project represents a tangible example of effective strategies for reducing an organization's carbon footprint.

To achieve this goal, a comprehensive data acquisition and monitoring system (DAQsystem) was created to collect information related to sustainability. This allows measuring the impact of various initiatives designed to enhance the building's sustainability. Real-time experimental measurements are recorded every 15 minutes for electricity and daily water consumption, ambient temperature, and relative humidity in every classroom. These readings will be displayed on a large screen located in the main hall during 2023–2024 (see Fig. 7.3). The system will be continuously upgraded as new measurements become available. It will be available to the ETSII community, allowing them to put forward new ideas for enhancement. The LivingLAB-ETSII DAQ system is accessible via an open access link,[1] which provides daily real-time public data on the building's energy performance and water consumption.

As an illustration of ETSII's engagement with the community, a hackathon entitled INDUSHack-LivingLabETSII was organized (UPV, 2023a). It lasted for 14 days in May 2023 and 42 students participated. Following the event, the innovative solutions and challenges suggested by students were thoroughly scrutinized, and the most feasible ones have been executed during the academic year. As another example, an awareness campaign on sustainability was launched. It consisted of numerous messages displayed on the ETSII's screens, transforming it into a virtual Agora.

Fig. 7.3. 5N Building at UPV That Is Part of the UPV Living Lab Experiment and View of the Screen Where the LivingLAB-ETSII DAQ System Will Be Displayed.

Source: The authors.

7. THE ROLE OF THE UNIVERSITY IN THE MISSION TRANSITION TEAM AND IN THE ENERGY TRANSITION BOARD

Further expanding upon the transformational dynamics within the university detailed in Section 3, we now turn our attention to the trends and initiatives unfolding at the niche level in the UPV ecosystem. One example of such active engagement is the UPV's integral involvement in the process facilitation and action research with the city, such as the Mission Transition Team (MTT). This type of action research contributes to the transformative ethos within the university, fostering a holistic approach that extends beyond administrative spheres.

Sustainability transitions and system transformations are flavored and accelerated when a diversity of system actors, who form dynamic networks with changing power relations over time, are involved (Avelino et al., 2016; Avelino & Wittmayer, 2016) and university can have a crucial intermediating role. These actors include those beyond the public administration, who typically do not participate in these processes. In this regard, and in the realm of a CUP for accelerating the València 2030 Climate Mission to achieve climate neutrality by 2030, the UPV assumed a pivotal role as an integral part of the MTT. The MTT is the group responsible for defining the preliminary objectives of the roadmap toward sustainability transition, conducting an analysis of the system in which it will operate, establishing the methodology, developing the stakeholder mapping and the list of actors, and planning and convening working sessions. This roadmap aims to be a clear and consensus-driven detailed strategy for accelerating the city's climate neutrality from a collective perspective.

The formation of these multi-stakeholder spaces and processes gives rise to the emergence of new initiatives from groups that often do not engage, for various reasons (e.g. lack of feedback), in traditional participatory processes (Frantzeskaki & Rok, 2018). This underscores the importance of experimentation and adopting a long-term perspective to mitigate the risks associated with short-term political considerations and achievement-based policies. The multi-stakeholder process goal is to co-create a roadmap that contains the considered steps necessary to achieve the sustainability transition of the city or system they are working with. The roadmap document can, and should, be seen as continually evolving and improving within the MTT. A standard structure for a "roadmap" should include at least the following content: (1) background of the system and issues to be addressed; (2) objectives of the process; (3) members and functions; (4) demonstrative projects with their respective tasks and responsible parties; and (5) a work plan and schedule for these projects.

In this regard, the universities bring a unique set of skills, expertise, intellectual capital, research capabilities, and commitment to academic values. They can also serve an intermediary role as a neutral facilitator for innovative co-creation processes at all stages (Fuenfschilling et al., 2019). The universities play a central role not only as hubs for innovation and problem-solving but also as facilitators, fostering effective communication and collaboration among diverse stakeholders. Furthermore, universities provide initial support, mediation, sustenance, and protection for collective experimentation.

In this context, the UPV collaborates with the city in a collective effort to co-create the roadmap for the València 2030 Climate Mission, drawing from the insights gained through the prior development of the city's 2030 Energy Transition Roadmap (Fig. 7.4). As a dedicated multi-stakeholder process was established for the energy sector, the Energy Transition Roundtable, engaged 24 stakeholders and 22 entities in a series of 29 sessions spanning over 2 years.

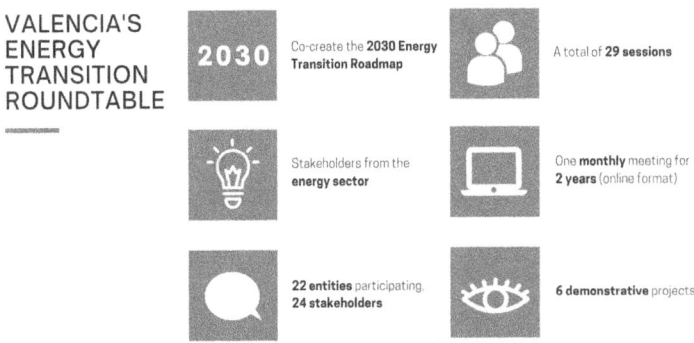

Fig. 7.4. Valencia 2030 Energy Transition Roadmap.[2]
Source: The authors.

The majority of these sessions took place through monthly online meetings and had as a result the Just and Inclusive Energy Transition Roundtable (Escario-Chust et al., 2023).

The previous experience illustrated the multi-faceted roles played by the academia in the process. The academia actively contributed as stakeholder but also as part of the steering group and facilitator team with two master students, three researchers and one professor (Fig. 7.5). The academia provided support in knowledge, methodology, internationalization, networking, and incorporating insights gained from ongoing reflexive monitoring research. In particular, the university team assumed a crucial role in safeguarding the process as a facilitator during practical sessions (Fig. 7.5), employing innovative methods rooted in systems thinking, design thinking (DT), and transition thinking (Gorissen et al., 2018). The adoption of this type of action research approach not only bolsters the transformative ethos within the university but also fosters a holistic perspective that transcends administrative changes in the university.

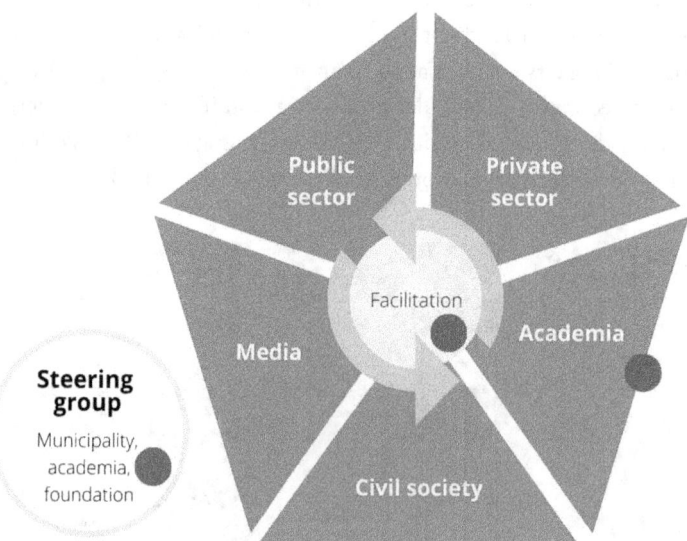

Fig. 7.5. University Role in the 2030 Energy Transition Roadmap in the City of València.

Source: The authors.

8. EDUCATION FOR JUST TRANSITIONS

As highlighted in Section 3, the transformation within the university is unfolding across various dimensions. Notably, at the niche level, within the educational landscape of UPV, we witness changes in the ethos of education, it extends to the very essence of education and its methods. This dynamic evolution is occurring in tandem with broader transformative at the landscape level (see Section 2).

The ongoing changes at the niche level reflect a concerted effort to align educational practices with the principles of a just transition. This involves cultivating transformative skills essential for individuals to contribute to institutions, society, and the workplace (Kordas et al., 2015). Additionally, the educational paradigm is adapting to equip individuals with capabilities to navigate complexity, uncertainty, and transdisciplinary problems (Lang et al., 2012; Lange, 2019). Recognizing the roots of ecological challenges in inequality and power imbalances, educational initiatives are designed to impart skills that address these core issues (Sultana, 2022).

As Ferrer-Balas et al. (2009) assert, the integration of sustainability into university activities, encompassing curriculum, research, and operations, is insufficient. The real challenge lies in integrating the university into the broader transformations of social systems. In response to this imperative and to transcend conventional academic practices, our proposal begins at the heart of the university – inside the classroom with young students (Aránguiz et al., 2020).

Our research journey has unveiled specific educational experiences where DT emerges as a powerful problem-solving approach for just sustainability transitions within the classroom. DT, with its alternating divergent and convergent thinking processes, provides an iterative reasoning framework. This allows educators and students alike to venture beyond traditional solutions, addressing complex, real-world problems creatively (Buchanan, 1992).

In three distinct educational instances with UPV's Master Degree in International Cooperation, drawing on critical design approaches (DiSalvo, 2022), systemic design (Sevaldson & Jones, 2019), and just transitions (Heffron, 2021) we engaged young students in a pedagogical assembly. Inspired by Latour (2007), this assembly entwined various individuals and entities within a co-design process.

In the first case (Aránguiz et al., 2020), students collaborated with members of UPV's Agroecological Market (AM) of the Vera Campus. They addressed challenges in the AM through action research, project-based learning (PBL), and DT. Our research revealed that PBL facilitated critical thinking (CT) in three categories: (i) critical self-reflection; (ii) critical action; and (iii) critical attitude toward reality, fostering reasoning and analytical skills (Aránguiz et al., 2020).

The second case aimed to explore how a pedagogical approach based on DT, care practices, and just transitions contributes to justice-oriented relational learning. Our findings demonstrated that this approach led to justice-oriented relational learning through five categories: place-based learning, prior learning, embodied learning, collaborative teamwork, and intersectionality (Aránguiz et al., forthcoming).

Finally, the third case explored a bi-directional (district–university–district) teaching-learning process for community problem-solving. This was facilitated by DT and action learning methodologies, collectively developed by students and community members of the Orriols district in the city of Valencia. Preliminary results indicate that the pedagogical proposal contributed to transdisciplinary learning in students while promoting a more just and sustainable urban transition for the migrant population of the Orriols district.

Within these educational experiences, we find ourselves at the intersection of critical design approaches and systemic design, illustrating the intricate interplay between education, social justice, city dynamics, and societal systems. Through a pedagogical assembly with young students, a collaborative weaving of various elements ensues, entangling people, places, temporalities, institutions, non-governmental organizations, grassroots organizations, farmers, practitioners, students, and researchers in a co-design process.

In conclusion, this exploration into education for a just transition within the university reflects a profound understanding of the interconnectedness of the landscape-niche and CUP. As transformations occur on different levels, a more just and sustainable society emerges. The approach involves breaking down barriers and adopting transdisciplinary, bottom-up teaching and learning methodologies to effectively address the root causes of sustainability problems that afflict our societies.

9. UNICITIES2030: STUDENT FOCUSED COLLABORATION IN THE CUPS

Within the intricate fabric of the CUP in Valencia, the UniCITIES2030 project emerges as a beacon, illuminating the path to amplify collaboration between academic inquiry and pragmatic urban governance (REDS, 2023) and contributing to provide insights for the binomial development. Supported by the Ministry of Universities of the Spanish Government, the project has been meticulously coordinated by REDS-USDN, with the active participation of Valencia and Vitoria cities as pilot cases during its inaugural edition.

UniCITIES2030 represents more than a project; it embodies a paradigm shift in collaborative experimentation, where academia and city governance converge to address the tangible needs of urban environments. At its core, the project propels the development of student theses, spanning from Bachelor to Master, intricately aligned with the actual needs of cities. The pilot phase in Valencia has already witnessed the initiation of co-creation sessions focused on defining student projects. This collaborative effort spans seven key areas of interest: innovation & technology, mobility & transport, renaturalization & biodiversity, resilience, energy, economy & industry, and social and citizen involvement.

UniCITIES2030 transcends the confines of specific objectives; it aspires to craft a robust methodology, laying the groundwork for future replication across diverse cities in Spain. This collaborative endeavor aims to transform cities into living laboratories, where innovative ideas and prototypes are tested, generating concrete evidence for sustainable urban transformation.

In essence, UniCITIES2030 represents a transformative spirit that transcends conventional boundaries of academic research and urban governance. As the project unfolds, it serves as a testament to the potential of collaborative initiatives, acting as a catalyst for a new era of sustainable and resilient cities shaped by the seamless synergy of academia and practical urban governance.

10. DISCUSSION

10.1. Key Dimensions for Propelling the CUP

This chapter intricately unfolds the narrative of a collaborative university project (CUP) in Valencia, driven by the transformative momentum of the Net-Zero Cities Mission spearheaded by the EU. Throughout the presented experiences, the exploration illuminates diverse dimensions through which the CUP fosters a mutually enriching collaboration between the city of València and the UPV.

In its primary facet, the CUP operates as a formidable knowledge powerhouse, aligning seamlessly with the principles articulated in urban sustainability transformation studies (Keeler et al., 2023). Envisaged in the formal agreement, the CUP actively *contributes specific knowledge and research crucial for the city's development model*. This collaborative knowledge production becomes pivotal in addressing challenges defined by the city, laying the foundation for a responsive and informed urban governance structure. Within this realm, the role of the chairs co-financed by the municipality is pivotal, focusing on areas defined by the municipality itself. This targeted research and knowledge production are channeled toward addressing specific challenges outlined by city representatives. The ongoing process involves mapping various existing university initiatives, showcasing the continuous evolution of the collaborative efforts. Beyond merely providing knowledge, the CUP, as illustrated by the Alliance of UPV Chairs, extends its impact to contribute to a deeper understanding of the concept and contents of the mission approach itself. This is exemplified by the organization of the Grand Debate and the definition of multiple pathways for the mission's development at the university, enriching the understanding of diverse options available to a university embracing the climate mission.

In a secondary dimension, the CUP serves as *a catalyst for experimentation and innovation in urban policies*, resonating with the imperative for transformative change crucial for sustainable development (Caughman et al., 2020). Notably, the Energy Transition Board and the Living Lab of the UPV spearhead initiatives related to energy efficiency, sustainable drainage systems, and daily routines in office buildings. These real experimentation practices create an environment for co-creation, exploration, and evaluation of innovations, promising iterative learning processes directed toward sustainable impact.

In a tertiary realm, the CUP emerges as a *vital educational space*, challenging prevailing ontologies, epistemologies, and methodologies in higher education. It aims to move beyond "academia as usual" (McGeown & Barry, 2023) by reconfiguring how we think about knowledge acquisition and learning. This emphasis on transdisciplinary education and action-oriented learning aligns with contemporary needs for professionals navigating the complexities of sustainability transitions.

In the fourth term, the UPV Living Lab project materializes the *university campuses* as transformative hubs, exemplifying innovation and climate neutrality within the city's physical space. Through initiatives implemented in the Vera Campus, solutions are tested on the ground, with the potential for replication in other neighborhoods of València. The holistic perspective of achieving climate neutrality within a whole engineering school stands out as a noteworthy initiative within the UPV Living Lab.

In the fifth term, it is important to recognize how the CUP and the UPV *reinforce the legitimacy* of the city's climate initiative. The university not only provides substantial support but also exercises clear leadership within its sphere of action. Its contributions extend to legitimizing innovative approaches in defining roadmaps and demonstrative projects, fostering a sense of realism and achievability for the ambitious goal of achieving city climate neutrality by 2030. This narrative, paints a vivid picture of the transformative role played by the CUP in Valencia, showcasing how collaborative efforts with the UPV significantly advance the goals of the Net-Zero Cities Mission. The CUP emerges not only as a conduit for knowledge and innovation but also as a critical player in shaping the future sustainability of the city.

10.2. Key Insights and Transformative Dynamics

In our exploration of the CUP in Valencia, we *showed that to create a well-functioning CUP, actions must be taken at different levels, aligning with the MLP framework.*

In dissecting and understanding the reasons behind functional CUP, the MLP is paramount (Geels, 2002; Geels & Schot, 2007; Smith et al., 2010). As Geels posits, transitions should evolve through the interplay of three levels: the regime, niches, and the landscape.

In the context of Valencia CUP, the commitment to becoming a carbon-neutral campus by 2030 resonates with the broader landscape-level challenges at the city level (Section 2) aligning with global warming concerns and the climate emergency.

At the regime level, the transformative elements within UPV, such as the creation of sustainability alliances through chairs and the mission orientation of the Vice-Rectorate of Sustainable Development with its Living Labs initiatives, mirror the regime destabilization necessary for sustainable transitions (Geels & Schot, 2007). These initiatives act as strategic alliances shaping the established order in socio-technical systems, reflecting the regime concept within the MLP.

The niche-level initiatives, exemplified by the Energy Transition Multi-Stakeholder Board and just transition education ethos, align with the niche spaces where innovators experiment with alternatives (Geels, 2002). UPV, as a living lab for experimentation, plays a pivotal role in the experimentation crucial for decarbonization efforts, echoing the niche concept in the MLP (Geels, 2002; Smith et al., 2010).

Furthermore, we showed here the catalyzing role of mission in the CUP creation and functioning. The EU's Net-Zero Cities Mission acted as a catalyst for the transformative journey of UPV, shaping the landscape-level challenges and providing a broader context for the university's commitment to carbon neutrality. This aligns with the literature on mission-oriented innovation and sustainability transitions, where overarching missions become catalysts for systemic change (Geels, 2002; Mazzucato, 2018).

The mission-oriented approach, particularly the commitment to becoming a carbon-neutral campus by 2030, acts as a catalytic force, guiding UPV's transformative trajectory. Notably, the Vice-Rectorate's dedicated focus on the mission, coupled with the establishment of living labs, reflects a deliberate and strategic alignment with mission-oriented goals. These initiatives become integral components of UPV's mission-oriented journey.

In conclusion, UPV's transformative journey within the CUP is intricately linked to a mission-oriented approach, catalyzed by the EU's Net-Zero Cities Mission. The initiatives at different analytical levels, as discussed through the lens of MLP, underscore the university's responsiveness to global challenges and its pivotal role in steering the city toward a sustainable and resilient future. The EU's mission acts as a driving force, providing a strategic context for UPV's commitment to sustainable transitions (Geels, 2002; Mazzucato, 2018).

11. CONCLUSIONS

In closing the pages of this chapter, the compelling narrative of the CUP in Valencia unfolds as a beacon of inspiration, guided by the transformative force of a mission-oriented approach sparked by the EU's Net-Zero Cities Mission.

Our exploration has delved into the complex relationship between city and university, revealing the multi-faceted dimensions through which the Valencian CUP becomes a driving force for symbiotic development. From the knowledge powerhouse shaping the city's development model to the strategic alignment with the MLP framework, each facet contributes to a holistic understanding of the partnership's significance.

Crucially, our journey into the València case study underscores the catalyzing role of mission in the CUP's creation and functioning. The EU's Net-Zero Cities Mission acts as the fuel, guiding the transformative trajectory of UPV and steering the city toward a sustainable and resilient future. This catalytic force, embedded in a commitment to becoming a carbon-neutral campus by 2030, highlights the mission-oriented innovation crucial for systemic change.

As the València case stands testament to the achievements of a singular partnership, it also emerges as a blueprint for global urban centers navigating the intricate path toward climate neutrality. The insights garnered from this exploration extend beyond the Valencian landscape, contributing to a broader dialogue on the transformative potential of CUPs. This chapter, therefore, not only encapsulates the Valencian journey but also serves as a roadmap, offering valuable lessons and strategies for cities worldwide in their pursuit of sustainable and climate-resilient futures.

- *Combination of high-level institutional frameworks and bottom-up initiatives*: The synergistic interplay between high-level initiatives, exemplified by the EU Cities Mission, and grassroots efforts stands as a cornerstone for the success of CUPs. These high-level initiatives provide a framework and justification for local endeavors, acting as guiding principles. In this dynamic relationship, grassroots initiatives serve as the transformative fuel, propelling initiatives like CUPs to fruition. The high-level frameworks set the stage, while the grassroots efforts infuse energy, resulting in a symbiotic collaboration that is essential for the success of transformative urban projects.
- *Diversify actions and transformations in the different levels*: The imperative to diversify actions, spanning various levels such as niches, regime, and landscape, resonates with arguments emphasizing the importance of experimentation in sustainable transitions. It's a strategic approach that acknowledges the complexity of urban systems and the need for multi-faceted interventions to address diverse challenges.
- *Build upon existing foundations*: The Valencian experience emphasizes the strategic value of building upon existing initiatives. This process involves a thorough evaluation of current initiatives, redirecting them toward desired goals, and uniting them under a common umbrella. Analogous to managing a diversified portfolio, this approach leverages institutional support, exemplified by the EU mission, as a pivotal instrument in steering existing initiatives toward transformative outcomes. This strategic redirection not only optimizes existing resources but also aligns with the broader discourse on sustainability transitions that emphasizes the significance of adaptive reuse and leveraging established systems.
- *Foster a culture of collaboration*: Encouraging a new culture of collaboration, where actors transcend their institutional roles to contribute to a shared "mission," becomes a driving force for meaningful transformation. This cultural shift aligns with the broader discourse on the need for transformative change and the evolving role of collaborative governance. The departure from the conventional norms of "academia as usual" and

"municipality as usual," as highlighted in our exploration, underscores the transformative potential embedded in collaborative and boundary-crossing approaches.

However, this narrative is not a conclusion but an ongoing contribution to the academic dialogue on collaborative urban transformation. The Valencian experience provides a valuable case study, but its significance lies in the insights it contributes to broader discussions on sustainable urban development and CUP development. As we look ahead, the conversation must evolve through further research, drawing on diverse case studies and theoretical frameworks to unravel the full potential of CUPs and refine their role in shaping the urban landscapes of tomorrow.

In this way, our conclusions not only encapsulate the Valencian journey but also contribute to the ongoing scholarly dialogue, offering both insights and questions that beckon further exploration and discussion.

NOTES

1. http://livinglab.etsii.upv.es:80/public-dashboards/b823e4562a144a3aa37d2fba0da14e34

2. All the icons are sourced from Canva and are available for free commercial use according to the Free Content License.

REFERENCES

Allen, J. H., Beaudoin, F., & Gilden, B. (2017). Building powerful partnerships: Lessons from Portland's climate action collaborative. *Sustainability: The Journal of Record*, 10(5), 276–281.

Aránguiz, P., Palau-Salvador, G., Belda, A., & Peris, J. (2020). Critical thinking using project-based learning: The case of the agroecological market at the "Universitat Politècnica de València". *Sustainability*, 12(9), 3553.

Aránguiz, P., Palau-Salvador, G., & Peris-Blanes, J. (2024). Design thinking for just transitions. Exploring relational and justice-oriented learning at the Universitat Politècnica de València, Spain. *International Journal of Sustainability in Higher Education*. Epub ahead of print April 4.

AtKisson, A. 2012. *Believing Cassandra: How to be an optimist in a pessimist's world*. Routledge.

Avelino, F., Wittmayer, J. M. (2016). Shifting power relations in sustainability transitions: A multi-actor perspective. *Journal of Environmental Policy & Planning*, 18(5), 628–649.

Avelino, F., Grin, J., Pel, B., & Jhagroe, S. (2016). The politics of sustainability transitions. *Journal of Environmental Policy & Planning*, 18(5), 557–567.

Ayuntamiento de València. (2023a). *Missions – Missions València 2030: Missions València 2030*. https://www.missionsvalencia.eu/missions/?lang=en

Ayuntamiento de València. (2023b). *The urban strategy home – Estrategia Urbana Valencia 2030*. https://estrategiaurbanavlc2030.es/en/

Buchanan, R. (1992). Wicked problems in design thinking. *Design Issues*, 8(2), 5–21.

Bulkeley, H. (2016). *Accomplishing climate governance*. Cambridge University Press.

Caughman, L., Beaudoin, F., & Keeler, L.W. (2023). The project–partnership cycle: Managing city–university partnerships for urban sustainability and resilience transformations. *Urban Transformations*, 5(1), 10. https://doi.org/10.1186/s42854-023-00055-x

Caughman, L., Keeler, L.W., & Beaudoin, F. (2020). Real-time evaluation of city–university partnerships for sustainability and resilience. *Sustainability*, 12(21), 8796.

DiSalvo, C. (2022). *Design as democratic inquiry: Putting experimental civics into practice*. MIT Press.

Dóci, G., Rohracher, H., & Kordas, O. (2022). Knowledge management in transition management: The ripples of learning. *Sustainable Cities and Society*, 78, 103621.

EC. (2021). *Climate-neutral and smart cities*. https://research-and-innovation.ec.europa.eu/funding/funding-opportunities/funding-programmes-and-open-calls/horizon-europe/eu-missions-horizon-europe/climate-neutral-and-smart-cities_en

EC. (2023). NextGenerationEU. https://commission.europa.eu/strategy-and-policy/eu-budget/eu-borrower-investor-relations/nextgenerationeu_en.

Escario-Chust, A., Vogelzang, F., Peris-Blanes, J., Palau-Salvador, G., & Segura-Calero, S. (2023). Can southern Europe lead an urban energy transition? Insights from the energy transition roundtable in Valencia, Spain. *Energy Research & Social Science*, 100, 103047.

European Commission. (2023, October 12). *Ten European cities awarded with EU Mission Label for their plans to reach climate-neutrality by 2030* [Press release]. https://ec.europa.eu/commission/presscorner/detail/en/IP_23_4879

Ferrer-Balas, D., Buckland, H., & de Mingo, M. (2009). Explorations on the university's role in society for sustainable development through a systems transition approach. Case-study of the Technical University of Catalonia (UPC). *Journal of Cleaner Production*, 17(12), 1075–1085.

Flor, A., Grin, J., Pel, B., & Jhagroe, J. (2016). The politics of sustainability transitions. *Journal of Environmental Policy & Planning*, 18(5), 557–567.

Flor, V., & Wittmayer, J. M. (2016). Shifting power relations in sustainability transitions: A multi-actor perspective. *Journal of Environmental Policy & Planning*, 18(5), 628–649.

Frantzeskaki, N., & Rok, A. (2018). Co-producing urban sustainability transitions knowledge with community, policy and science. *Environmental Innovation and Societal Transitions*, 29, 47–51.

Fuenfschilling, L., Frantzeskaki, N., & Coenen, L. (2019). Urban experimentation & sustainability transitions. *European Planning Studies*, 27(2), 219–228.

Geels, F. W. (2002). Technological transitions as evolutionary reconfiguration processes: A multi-level perspective and a case-study. *Research Policy*, 31(8), 1257–1274.

Geels, F. W., & Schot, J. (2007). Typology of sociotechnical transition pathways. *Research Policy*, 36(3), 399–417.

Gorissen, L., Spira, F., Meynaerts, E., Valkering, P., & Frantzeskaki, N. (2018). Moving towards systemic change? Investigating acceleration dynamics of urban sustainability transitions in the Belgian city of Genk. *Journal of Cleaner Production*, *173*, 171–185.

Guerrieri, M., La Gennusa, M., Peri, G., Rizzo, G., & Scaccianoce, G. (2019). University campuses as small-scale models of cities: Quantitative assessment of a low carbon transition path. *Renewable and Sustainable Energy Reviews*, *113*, 109263.

Heffron, R. J. (2021). What is the "just transition"? In *Achieving a just transition to a low-carbon economy* (pp. 9–19). Palgrave Macmillan.

Holmberg, J., Lundqvist, U., Svanström, M., & Arehag, M. (2012). The university and transformation towards sustainability: The strategy used at Chalmers University of Technology. *International Journal of Sustainability in Higher Education*, *13*(3), 219–231.

Keeler, L.W., Beaudoin, F., Cid, A., Cowley, R., Fahy, S., Lerner, A., Moran, C., & Torney, D. (2023). Building transformative city–university sustainability partnerships: The audacious partnerships process. *Urban Transformations*, *5*(1). 1. https://doi.org/10.1186/s42854-022-00045-5.

Keeler, L. W., Beaudoin, F., Wiek, A., John, B., Lerner, A. M., Beecroft, R., Tamm, K., Seebacher, A., Lang, D. J., & Kay, B. (2019). Building actor-centric transformative capacity through city–university partnership. *Ambio*, *48*, 529–538.

Kordas, O, Pereverza, K., Pasichnyi, O., & Nikiforovich, E. (2015). Developing skills for sustainability change agents with a participatory backcasting teaching toolbox. In S. Nesbit & T. M. Froese (Eds.), *Proceedings of EESD15: The 7th conference on engineering education for sustainable development*, University of British Columbia, Vancouver, Canada. June 9–12.

Kumdokrub, T., Carson, S., & You, F. (2023). Cornell university campus metabolism and circular economy using a living laboratory approach to study major resource and material flows. *Journal of Cleaner Production*, *421*, 138469.

Lang, D. J., Wiek, A., Bergmann, M., Stauffacher, M., Martens, P., Moll, P., Swilling, M., & Thomas, C. J. (2012). Transdisciplinary research in sustainability science: Practice, principles, and challenges. *Sustainability Science*, *7*, 25–43.

Lange, E. A. (2019). Transformative learning for sustainability. In W. F. Leal (Ed.), *Encyclopedia of sustainability in higher education* (pp. 1954–1966). Springer.

Latour, B. (2007). *Reassembling the social: An introduction to actor–network-theory*. OUP Oxford.

Leal, F. W., & Bardi, U. (Eds.). (2019). *Sustainability on university campuses: Learning, skills building and best practices*. Springer.

Mazzucato, M. (2018). *Mission-oriented research & innovation in the European: A problem-solving approach to fuel innovation-led growth.*

McGeown, C., & Barry, J. (2023). Agents of (un) sustainability: Democratising universities for the planetary crisis. *Frontiers in Sustainability, 4*, 1166642.

REDS. (2023). *UnicitiES2030* [Blog]. https://reds-sdsn.es/unicities2030/

Sevaldson, B., & Jones, P. (2019). An interdiscipline emerges: Pathways to systemic design. *She Ji: The Journal of Design, Economics, and Innovation, 5*(2), 75–84.

Smith, A., Voß, J.-P., & Grin, J., (2010). Innovation studies and sustainability transitions: The allure of the multi-level perspective and its challenges. *Research Policy, 39*, 435–448.

Soberón, M., Ezquerra-Lázaro, I., Sánchez-Chaparro, T., Moreno-Serna, J., Dóci, G., & Kordas, O. (2023). Supporting municipalities to develop collaboration capability to facilitate urban transitions and sustainability: Role of transition intermediaries in Madrid. *Journal of Cleaner Production, 426*, 138964.

Sultana, F. (2022). Critical climate justice. *The Geographical Journal, 188*(1), 118–124.

Tian, X., Zhou, Y., Morris, B., & You, F. (2022). Sustainable design of Cornell University campus energy systems toward climate neutrality and 100% renewables. *Renewable and Sustainable Energy Reviews, 161*, 112383.

UN-Habitat. (2016). *The new urban agenda illustrated handbook*. UN-Habitat. https://unhabitat.org/the-new-urban-agenda-illustrated

UPV. (2022a). *12 cátedras de la UPV lanzan La Gran Encuesta sobre la neutralidad en carbono de la Universitat Politècnica de València.* Catedrades [Blog]. https://catedrades.webs.upv.es/12-catedras-de-la-upv-lanzan-la-gran-encuesta-sobre-la-neutralidad-en-carbono-de-la-universitat-politecnica-de-valencia/.

UPV. (2022b). *Noticia UPV: La UPV y València Quieren Ser Neutras En Carbono y Por Ello Han Impulsado Las Jornadas La Alianza UPV – Ciudad Para La Misión Climática València 2030.* Universitat Politècnica de València. https://www.upv.es/noticias-upv/noticia-13835-alcanzar-la-ne-es.html.

UPV. (2023a). *ETSII Valencia.* https://www.etsii.upv.es/noticia-es.php?id=1073.

UPV. (2023b). *UPV living lab – Introduction.* VCAMPUS. https://www.upv.es/entidades/vcampus/en/en-living-lab/.

UPV. (2023c). *Urban energy transition chair.* Cátedra de Transición Energética Urbana. https://catenerg.webs.upv.es/en/home-2/

UPV. (2023d). *VCAMPUS.* https://www.upv.es/entidades/vcampus/en/start/.

Westley, F., Tjornbo, O., Schultz, L., Olsson, P., Folke, C., Crona, B., & Bodin, O. (2013). A theory of transformative agency in linked social-ecological systems. *Ecology and Society, 18*(3), 27. https://doi.org/10.5751/ES-05072-180327

World Design Organization. (2019, September 9). *Valencia named world design capital 2022* [Press release]. https://wdo.org/valencia-named-world-design-capital-2022/s

8

NATIONAL PLATFORMS TO TRANSFORM CITIES USING COLLECTIVE EXPERIMENTATION AND SCALE: THE CASE OF SWEDEN AND SPAIN

Jaime Moreno-Serna[a], Olga Kordas[b],
Julio Lumbreras[a], Åsa Minoz[b], Nayla Saniour[a]
and Harald Rohracher[c]

[a]*Universidad Politécnica de Madrid, Spain*
[b]*KTH Royal Institute of Technology, Sweden*
[c]*Linköping University, Sweden*

ABSTRACT

With the overarching need for deep urban transformations worldwide, national platforms for cities have been emerging over the past few years in several European countries as a useful framework to support and unify the work that cities have been doing individually. In particular, Sweden and Spain have been two of the first countries where a National Cities Mission Platform has emerged, namely Viable Cities and citiES 2030. This chapter explores the emergence of these convening and intermediary vehicles, the key enablers that allowed its formation, and the rationale that consolidates it. It also delves into the distinctive value proposition of these platforms and their role in reinforcing multi-level and multi-stakeholder collaborations, facing silos in a national context, promoting cross-city stable interactions, aligning national and European initiatives toward the Cities Mission, and co-creating and consolidating the "next practices" of climate urban transitions.

Keywords: Intermediary organizations; climate city contracts; multi-city action; cities European mission; urban climate neutrality; learning and experimentation

INTRODUCTION

Cities play a crucial role in the transition toward sustainability due to their significant contribution to emissions and population well-being. Recognizing this, the European Commission has launched a Mission to achieve 100 climate-neutral cities by 2030, aligning with global agendas such as the 2030 Agenda, Habitat III, and the European Green Deal. However, achieving climate-neutral cities requires more than just a vision; it demands concrete actions that encompass diverse stakeholders and sectors, translating vision into implementation (Hodson & Marvin, 2010; Kemp et al., 2007; Loorbach et al., 2015). This mission-driven approach aligns innovation toward addressing societal challenges, a concept echoed in historical missions such as the moon landing, which catalyzed extensive technological advancements, highlighting the transformative potential of such endeavors (Mulgan, 2009).

Implementing mission-oriented strategies requires clear, ambitious, and measurable goals that engage both citizens and industries while allowing freedom in approach and bottom-up solutions (Mazzucato, 2017). Such missions do not dictate the path to success but stimulate a range of interconnected initiatives, demanding a systemic approach involving interdisciplinary academic work, collaborations across industries, and innovative public–private partnerships (Mazzucato, 2016). Yet, realizing these missions poses multi-faceted challenges, necessitating prolonged collaboration among diverse actors, including public, private, and civil society, fostering new forms of partnership and resource allocation (Mazzucato, 2018, 2019).

Moreover, a mission-oriented approach requires a shift in governance and culture, emphasizing collaboration among sectors and the active engagement of citizens. This entails establishing multi-actor collaboration spaces, instituting regulatory sandboxes, and fostering innovation ecosystems while investing in the education and training of individuals working across various organizations (Armenakis et al., 2011; Mazzucato, 2019). Implementing missions involves creating stable multi-actor collaboration spaces, incentivizing, educating, connecting with citizens, and coordinating among actors, making it imperative to ponder and refine the mission implementation process for effective outcomes.

THE NEED FOR NATIONAL CONVENING STRUCTURES IN THE EU CLIMATE-NEUTRAL CITIES MISSION

Cities have increasingly assumed a central role in implementing missions toward climate neutrality and greater sustainability. Despite limited power in shaping new regulations or laws, they are close to citizens and local businesses and can use soft forms of governance to facilitate change, create visions of a more sustainable future, and coordinate with other levels of government. There has been a long tradition of collaborative city networks, including C40, ICLEI, Eurocities, Energy Cities, ERRIN, and others. While these networks certainly have contributed to learning between cities, they have been too informal and loosely coupled to coordinate the implementation of mission-oriented policies. To achieve such mission goals, new national platforms for the collaboration of cities, the joint development and testing of new instruments, and the coordination between urban and national actors have been established in different countries, as we will describe further below. This idea has also been taken up for the implementation of the European Union (EU) Cities Mission, where the European Commission has created a one-stop-shop platform called NetZeroCities,[1] connecting several of these networks and including other partners to support EU-selected cities in their mission and offering a comprehensive suite of innovative climate policy tools. Despite the advantages these networks offer, each city operates within its unique national context, significantly shaping its operational strategies and approaches.

The emergence of the National Cities Mission Platforms stands as a transformative approach (Austin & Seitanidi, 2012; Waddock, 2020), steering away from individual city efforts toward collective action within a country. These platforms cultivate a community of practice among municipal officials, fostering spaces for knowledge exchange, mutual learning, and joint efforts aimed at significant urban transformations, particularly using decarbonization as the main lever to transform the city.

Acknowledging the limitations of individual city endeavors in addressing interconnected challenges such as climate change and systemic injustice, these innovative platforms advocate for collaboration among cities within the same country. By leveraging shared knowledge, regulatory similarities, and cultural affinities, they aim to effectively confront "wicked" problems.

The establishment of National Cities Mission Platforms signifies an important shift in urban transformations, emphasizing deep collaboration, shared learning, and collective action across multiple cities within a country. These platforms serve as pivotal elements in driving ambitious sustainability goals, mirroring the objectives outlined in initiatives like the EU Cities Mission, thereby reshaping the conventional approach to urban transitions and climate neutrality.

The design and implementation of these intermediary organizations present a considerable challenge due to the absence of a well-defined organizational archetype and a predominant focus on project execution rather than the cultivation of collaborative environments in funding efforts (Kanda et al., 2020; Soberón et al., 2022; Wolf et al., 2020). Universities are well positioned to initiate these platforms, as will be exemplified later. They can fulfill a synergistic function, particularly in the initial stages, leveraging their resources and close support to ensure sustained engagement from early stakeholders (Purcell, 2019). Moreover, universities, given their neutrality and convening power, can effectively align the platform's shared mandate with the interests of key city stakeholders (Ehlenz, 2016). This role strengthens the platform's ability to attract public attention, diverse actors, and resources. Additionally, universities significantly contribute by embedding legitimacy and knowledge capabilities into the platform's learning processes from the very start (Ehlenz, 2018; Ezquerra-Lázaro et al., 2021).

THE CREATION OF THE FIRST NATIONAL PLATFORMS

Among the various national support structures, two platforms stand out for their pre-existing groundwork before the mission's launch: Viable Cities in Sweden and citiES 2030 in Spain. These platforms serve as dynamic catalysts for collaborative change, uniting cities, industry, academia, and civil society. With a shared vision targeting climate-neutral cities by 2030, they symbolize a collective pursuit of systemic transformation, advocating for social, ecological, and economic sustainability within the confines of global planetary boundaries. Viable Cities,[2] initiated by the Royal Institute of Technology (KTH) in collaboration with public and private entities, inspired citiES 2030, which took root within the Technical University of Madrid (UPM) and gained support from the incorporation of the Climate Knowledge Innovation Community (EIT Climate-KIC) as co-promoters of the platform.

Both Viable Cities and citiES 2030 emerged from a grassroots, cohesive effort, leveraging the neutrality and prestige of the universities driving them, supported by the trust of key individuals. However, from the outset, they sought top-down legitimization, receiving endorsement and resources from the central government to facilitate their respective activities. In the case of Viable Cities, various Swedish national agencies like the Innovation Agency, Sustainable Development Agency, and Energy Agency played this role. For citiES 2030,[3] it was the Ministry of Science and Innovation and the Spanish Directorate for Climate Change under the Ministry for Ecological Transition that provided initial support. Both platforms capitalized on their intermediation capacity to enhance alignment between local and national climate policies and the innovations proposed by the European Cities Mission.

Similar initiatives are emerging across Europe, notably in countries like Romania (where M100 platform has recently launched), Austria, Portugal, Greece, France, Italy, and the Netherlands. Furthermore, universities and local entities in other regions, such as Ukraine and Latin America, are closely observing these developments, aiming to fortify their local transitions toward climate neutrality. The cases of citiES 2030 and Viable Cities are then analyzed to share lessons learned and inspire other mission-based innovation initiatives.

CASE STUDY: VIABLE CITIES AND CITIES 2030

Both programs undertake a wide array of activities. Below are descriptions of some of the most relevant ones that have fostered cross-pollination, analyzing the role of the university in each of them.

The *Transition Lab Within Viable Cities* serves as a strategic initiative aimed at consolidating a wide community among the 23 cities engaged in the program. It serves as a stable space to disseminate transformative changes by nurturing trust among key stakeholders, aligning their missions toward climate neutrality, and promoting ongoing interaction (Austin & Seitanidi, 2012).

Comprising a series of interconnected events, tools, and methods, the Transition Lab[4] operates on foundational principles that distinguish its approach: (i) activities encompass broader processes rather than isolated events, (ii) collaboration involves stakeholders from academia, public institutions, industry, and civil society, emphasizing diverse engagement through a multi-level and 4-helix approach, (iii) it is based on shared interests, fostering an inclusive and enabling collaborative environment, (iv) while technical specifics are vital, emphasis remains on inspiring content over mere logistical details, and (v) balancing technical topics with motivational content.

A primary objective of the Transition Lab is to facilitate reflective learning among cities and pertinent actors, enhancing their capacities for transition management, citizen involvement, innovative methodologies, and novel financial models. KTH and the other academic organizations comprising Viable Cities provide legitimacy to Transition Labs and thanks to their convening capacity these events have been consolidated as crucial mechanisms to foster collaboration, knowledge exchange, and collective learning toward sustainable urban transformations in Sweden.

Climate city contracts (CCC) are an innovative governance tool aimed at channeling broad political commitment at various levels (municipalities, regions, states, and the European Commission), fostering the development of sufficiently ambitious, inclusive, and economically viable municipal action plans (Shabb & McCormick, 2023). They also aim to ensure the continued participation of key actors from the private, social, and academic sectors in each territory.

First launched by Viable Cities in 2020, these contracts are reviewed annually with renewed commitments. Presently, in Sweden, 23 cities are signing these contracts between municipalities and various government agencies affiliated with Viable Cities, under the auspices of the European Commission and coordinated through Viable Cities platform (which also includes its own commitments). The CCCs combine clear political commitments toward climate neutrality, a set of specific measures to realize these commitments, a realistic estimation of costs and potential financing for the climate transition in each city, as well as a group of local stakeholders serving as change agents (Shabb & McCormick, 2023).

This initiative was adopted in 2021 by citiES 2030,[5] and since then, Spanish cities have initiated their commitment processes and systemic planning for the climate transition in collaboration with the Ministry for Ecological Transition. In 2022, the European Commission, through the Net Zero Cities platform, launched this instrument for all cities involved in the mission. Viable Cities emphasizes the importance of the process over the document itself, focusing on its iterative nature. Thanks to the CCCs, in addition to refining and concretely grounding commitments and plans, new operational structures have been established as interdepartmental teams in municipalities, integrating key government areas such as urban planning, mobility, education, culture, environment, economy, finance, etc. Another important outcome of CCCs is the co-legitimation of the mission-oriented climate work in each city, creating new policies far beyond specific political contexts. Due to its scientific and interdisciplinary nature, the entities forming the Viable Cities' program office have been able to reinforce this process with knowledge and capabilities in fields such as finance, urban planning, or stakeholder management (Shabb & McCormick, 2023).

Apart from supporting the development of CCCs, citiES 2030 offers three types of services[6] to the multiple stakeholders that are members of the platform: (i) networking; (ii) training; and (iii) implementation capabilities.

One of the main training initiatives launched by citiES 2030 is a *summer course*[7] designed to bring together individuals from key stakeholders of cities within the platform (currently 17). This course, held in collaboration with the Menendez Pelayo International University in Santander, creates a neutral and deeply inspiring environment with its facilities situated in an inspirational coastal setting.

The summer course attracts over a hundred participants, including around ten technical and managerial officials from each city. Emphasizing interactive and continuous learning approaches, the course focuses on fostering trust, commitment, and communication skills. This stands in contrast to more traditional perspectives that view capacity building as an individual process of acquiring knowledge (Dóci et al., 2022; Soberón et al., 2023). Prior to the course, participants engage in virtual onboarding sessions to introduce them to the topics they will explore.

In the 2023 edition, each day was dedicated to cross-cutting themes: (i) climate futures, political commitments, and citizen engagement, (ii) effective commitments and private sector financing instruments, and (iii) city collaboration and partnerships. According to climate policy leaders from several cities within citiES 2030, this course enables them to "embrace a new paradigm of work and collaboration among cities, prioritizing learning over dogmas, emphasizing processes and the quality of human relationships, taking collective risks rather than individual ones, and perceiving themselves as modest actors facing complex challenges." Additionally, the course contributes to the belief that

> *this multi-stakeholder platform works, it is beneficial, it unites and supports us, enabling us to achieve much more together. Having diverse actors from multiple sectors provides the opportunity to communicate needs, what they require from the Mission, and demonstrates their high interest in materializing commitments into concrete projects.*[8]

Leveraging the UPM's expertise in creating communities of practice through educational tools like MOOCs or Masters, and the established academic and structural innovations created around its Center for Innovation in Technology for Human Development, itdUPM (Moreno Serna et al., 2022), the summer course program has focused on promoting organizational learning. This facilitates the enhancement of existing practices and the implementation of new interdepartmental structures and systemic work approaches (Soberón et al., 2023). A crucial aspect involves addressing the personal dimension of collaborative relationships, an aspect often overlooked in literature focused on organizational relationships (Soberón et al., 2023).

Another noteworthy initiative of citiES 2030 to build implementation capabilities is a *multi-city program* involving the seven Spanish Mission cities: Madrid, Barcelona, Valencia, Seville, Zaragoza, Valladolid, and Vitoria. This initiative stemmed from the desire of each city's key officials in climate policy to build a joint program, unprecedented in local Spanish climate action. The program is centered on energy-efficient housing rehabilitation, and aims to renovate a total of one million homes across all cities in the coming years. Through this initiative, the transformative portfolio approach (Bögel et al., 2019; Wolfram et al., 2019) is being put into practice with concrete projects. To address regulatory challenges, lack of capacity, and the need for innovation in financial instruments, all cities are concurrently working on change levers associated with organizational, regulatory, and social aspects.

The program focuses on reducing energy consumption, including using innovative solutions like bio-based materials, enhancing energy efficiency, and strengthening local capacities. Each city has specific activities tailored to its context, such as energy-efficient construction in Madrid, Sevilla, Valencia, Valladolid, and Vitoria-Gasteiz, public–private collaboration for affordable housing in Barcelona, and emissions reduction through renewable energy communities in Zaragoza. Thanks to the UPM's prior experience in action research and in the involvement of stakeholders working with vulnerable populations in Spain and globally, a just transition dimension is currently being developed to integrate the voices and needs of these collectives within the program.

This initiative aims to transform the construction industry by developing energy-efficient, circular materials while incorporating local energy generation and strengthening local markets. It emphasizes capacity building, enabling communities to engage economically and participate actively in the transition and climate challenges. The vision is comprehensive, targeting not only the built environment but also social and organizational structures, enhancing local capabilities, and sharing the benefits of this transition among communities.

CONCLUSIONS

In pursuit of climate-neutral cities by 2030, the EU's mission-driven approach underscores the transformative power of collaborative city networks and national convening structures. The emergence of National Cities Mission Platforms signifies a shift from individual city efforts to collective action within a country, fostering collaboration, shared learning, and joint urban transformations. Initiatives like Viable Cities and citiES 2030 exemplify grassroots endeavors leveraging university partnerships, steering transformative programs, and providing an example of how universities can reinforce orchestrating functions within this kind of intermediary organizations. Next, the main functions carried out by these national platforms are summarized, along with the roles that universities could play in strengthening them:

- *Creation of communities and strengthening interpersonal bonds* within cities and among cities, where universities, in addition to their traditional neutrality and legitimacy, can contribute to a new active role as unifying agents.
- *Development of ambitious commitments and strategic planning*, where universities, beyond expert knowledge, can contribute with interdisciplinary capabilities in areas such as climate finance, urban planning, or stakeholder management.
- *Capability building and mutual learning*, where universities can provide their educational innovative methodologies, particularly through experience-based learning programs.

- *Transformative action*, where universities can contribute by shifting from individual research projects to city-driven initiatives where interconnected learning informs actions based on city needs.
- *Multi-level alignment* in which universities can establish themselves as spaces for maintaining stable dialogue among highly diverse actors contributing to relational fabrics that share a long-term purpose.

Thanks to these functions, National Cities Mission Platforms can embody systemic approaches, facilitating innovative governance tools like CCCs and multi-city programs. Through these efforts, cities are addressing regulatory challenges, enhancing energy efficiency, and strengthening local capacities while nurturing collaborative ecosystems. Besides, universities can also benefit from participating in this kind of environment, preparing their communities, activating a shared purpose around new research and training programs with a strong social focus, and transforming themselves to better serve their third mission.

However, national platforms and universities that support them face big challenges such as the lack of recognizable previous examples of collaborative programs, funding schemes focused on execution, siloed-organizational structures, or difficulties for multi-level coordination. The emphasis on knowledge sharing, organizational learning, just transitions, and comprehensive visions may help to face these challenges and contribute to reshaping urban landscapes, promoting sustainability across societal, ecological, and economic dimensions. It is time to unlock our collective intelligence potential!

NOTES

1. https://netzerocities.eu/
2. https://viablecities.se/en/om/
3. https://cities2030.es/en/about/
4. https://viablecities.se/en/klimatneutrala-stader-2030/transition-lab/

5. https://diadespues.org/evento/barcelona-madrid-seville-and-valencia-accelerate-the-progress-towards-climate-neutrality/?lang=en

6. https://cities2030.es/en/servicios/

7. https://cities2030.es/en/curso-de-verano-2/

8. Quotes extracted from the summer course report, see: https://drive.google.com/file/d/1SDnJ9DurF61X-eCbHdAeG3Qt1IT5fVGa/view?usp=drive_link

REFERENCES

Armenakis, A., Brown, S., & Mehta, A. (2011). Organizational culture: Assessment and transformation. *Journal of Change Management*, 11(3), 305–328. https://doi.org/10.1080/14697017.2011.568949

Austin, J. E., & Seitanidi, M. M. (2012). Collaborative value creation: A review of partnering between nonprofits and businesses: Part I. Value creation spectrum and collaboration stages. *Nonprofit and Voluntary Sector Quarterly*, 41(5), 726–758.

Bögel, P., Pereverza, K., Upham, P., & Kordas, O. (2019). Linking socio-technical transition studies and organisational change management: Steps towards an integrative, multi-scale heuristic. *Journal of Cleaner Production*, 232, 359–368. https://doi.org/10.1016/j.jclepro.2019.05.286

Dóci, G., Rohracher, H., & Kordas, O. (2022). Knowledge management in transition management: The ripples of learning. *Sustainable Cities and Society*, 78, 103621. https://doi.org/10.1016/j.scs.2021.103621

Ehlenz, M. M. (2016). Neighborhood revitalization and the anchor institution: Assessing the impact of the University of Pennsylvania's West Philadelphia initiatives on university city. *Urban Affairs Review*, 52(5), 714–750.

Ehlenz, M. M. (2018). Defining university anchor institution strategies: Comparing theory to practice. *Planning Theory & Practice*, 19(1), 74–92.

Ezquerra-Lázaro, I., Gómez-Pérez, A., Mataix, C., Soberón, M., Moreno-Serna, J., & Sánchez-Chaparro, T. (2021). A dialogical approach to readiness for change towards sustainability in higher education institutions: The case of the SDGs seminars at the Universidad Politécnica de Madrid. *Sustainability, 13*(16), 9168.

Hodson, M., & Marvin, S. (2010). Can cities shape socio-technical transitions and how would we know if they were? *Research Policy, 39*(4), 477–485.

Kanda, W., Kuisma, M., Kivimaa, P., & Hjelm, O. (2020). Conceptualising the systemic activities of intermediaries in sustainability transitions. *Environmental Innovation and Societal Transitions, 36,* 449–465. https://doi.org/10.1016/j.eist.2020.01.002

Kemp, R., Loorbach, D., & Rotmans, J. (2007). Transition management as a model for managing processes of co-evolution towards sustainable development. *The International Journal of Sustainable Development & World Ecology, 14*(1), 78–91.

Loorbach, D., Frantzeskaki, N., & Lijnis Huffenreuter, R. (2015). Transition management: Taking stock from governance experimentation. *Journal of Corporate Citizenship, 2015*(58), 48–66. https://doi.org/10.9774/GLEAF.4700.2015.ju.00008

Mazzucato, M. (2016). From market fixing to market-creating: A new framework for innovation policy. *Industry and Innovation, 23*(2), 140–156.

Mazzucato, M. (2017). *Mission-oriented innovation policy* [Working paper]. UCL Institute for Innovation and Public Purpose. https://www.ucl.ac.uk/bartlett/public-purpose/sites/public-purpose/files/moip-challenges-and-opportunities-working-paper-2017-1.pdf

Mazzucato, M. (2018). *Mission-oriented research & innovation in the European Union.* European Commission. https://op.europa.eu/en/publication-detail/-/publication/5b2811d1-16be-11e8-9253-01aa75ed71a1/language-en

Mazzucato, M. (2019). *Governing missions in the European Union.* Independent Expert Report. https://research-and-innovation.ec.europa.eu/knowledge-publications-tools-and-data/publications/all-publications/governing-missions-european-union_en

Moreno Serna, J., Sánchez Chaparro, T., Mataix Aldeanueva, C., & Purcell, W. (2022). Driving transformational sustainability in a university through structural and academic innovation: A case study of a public university in Spain. *Advances in Engineering Education, 10*(1), Article 1.

https://advances.asee.org/driving-transformational-sustainability-in-a-university-through-structural-and-academic-innovation-a-case-study-of-a-public-university-in-spain/

Mulgan, G. (2009). *The art of public strategy: Mobilizing power and knowledge for the common good.* Oxford University Press on Demand.

Purcell, W. M. (2019). A conceptual framework of leadership and governance in sustaining entrepreneurial universities illustrated with case material from a retrospective review of a university's strategic transformation: The enterprise university. In T. Kliewe, T. Kesting, C. Plewa, & T. Baaken (Eds.), *Developing engaged and entrepreneurial universities* (pp. 243–260). Springer.

Shabb, K., & McCormick, K. (2023). Achieving 100 climate neutral cities in Europe: Investigating climate city contracts in Sweden. *Npj Climate Action, 2*(1), Article 1. https://doi.org/10.1038/s44168-023-00035-8

Soberón, M., Ezquerra-Lázaro, I., Sánchez-Chaparro, T., Moreno-Serna, J., Dóci, G., & Kordas, O. (2023). Supporting municipalities to develop collaboration capability to facilitate urban transitions and sustainability: Role of transition intermediaries in Madrid. *Journal of Cleaner Production, 426*, 138964. https://doi.org/10.1016/j.jclepro.2023.138964

Soberón, M., Sánchez-Chaparro, T., Smith, A., Moreno-Serna, J., Oquendo-Di Cosola, V., & Mataix, C. (2022). Exploring the possibilities for deliberately cultivating more effective ecologies of intermediation. *Environmental Innovation and Societal Transitions, 44*, 125–144. https://doi.org/10.1016/j.eist.2022.06.003

Waddock, S. (2020). Thinking transformational system change. *Journal of Change Management, 20*(3), 189–201. https://doi.org/10.1080/14697017.2020.1737179

Wolf, P., Harboe, J., Sudbrack Rothbarth, C., Gaudenz, U., Arsan, L., Obrist, C., & van Leeuwen, M. (2021). Non-governmental organisations and universities as transition intermediaries in sustainability transformations building on grassroots initiatives. *Creativity and Innovation Management, 30*(3), 596–618.

Wolfram, M., Borgström, S., & Farrelly, M. (2019). Urban transformative capacity: From concept to practice. *Ambio, 48*(5), 437–448. https://doi.org/10.1007/s13280-019-01169-y

ABOUT THE EDITORS

Julio Lumbreras, PhD, Eng, MPA, is Professor at the Technical University of Madrid and teaching at Harvard University, where he is the instructor of the course on "Sustainable Cities." He was a member of the Board of the European Mission for "Climate-neutral and Smart Cities." He is now part of the Net Zero Cities consortium, and he is coordinating the multi-stakeholder platform for the implementation of the mission in Spain (citiES 2030). He is founding Associate Editor in the *Open Access Journal on Frontiers in Sustainable Cities*. He is co-author of more than 80 papers and books on air quality, climate change, sustainable cities, and higher education. He is passionate about increasing sustainability in higher education, turning universities into key agents to systemically transform cities toward sustainability.

Jaime Moreno-Serna holds a PhD in Industrial Engineering from the Universidad Politécnica de Madrid (UPM), a Master's degree in Technologies for Development from UPM, a Master's degree in Environmental Engineering from the Ecole Nationale Supérieure de Techniques Avancées de Paris, and a Bachelor's degree in Industrial Engineering from UPM. He is an Assistant Professor in the Department of Organizational Engineering at UPM and collaborates with various teams and projects in education and applied research, with an interdisciplinary and multi-actor approach, to accelerate innovation in policies that facilitate the achievement of the Sustainable Development Goals. His research areas focus on the analysis of interorganizational environments from the perspective of multi-stakeholder partnerships, transitions toward sustainability, and collaborative leadership.

ABOUT THE CONTRIBUTORS

Jose Luis Alapont is a PhD Architect and Associate Professor of Architectural Design at the Universitat Politècnica de València (UPV). He is currently the Office Director of Green Transition, working on the development of the university's strategy to achieve carbon neutrality. He is in charge of the UPV Living Lab. His research focuses on industrialized systems for sustainable and eco-efficient renovation of buildings and sustainable strategies for zero-carbon neighbors.

Jordi Peris Blanes is Professor at the Department of Engineering Projects at the Universitat Politècnica de València(UPV). In addition, he is Researcher at INGENIO CSIC-UPV center. His research interests combine sustainability transitions, innovation studies, and urban transformations. He has been Deputy Major of Valencia City Council and General Coordinator of Urban Strategies and Sustainable Agenda.

Sergio Segura Calero has a PhD in Geography from the University of Seville. Since 2019, he has been a Postdoctoral Researcher at the INGENIO institute (CSIC-UPV), at the Polytechnic University of Valencia (UPV), Spain. Holding a Master's degree in Territorial and Local Development Planning and Management, he specializes in Demographic, Economic, and Social Statistics. He brings extensive scientific and teaching experience in Spatial Planning and Transition to Sustainability, emphasizing a territorial and urban focus. His active involvement in numerous national and international projects reflects his orientation toward action, participation, transdisciplinarity, and knowledge co-production.

Juan Camilo Cardenas is Professor of Economics at the University of Massachusetts Amherst, USA, and the Universidad de los Andes in Colombia. He earned his PhD in Resource and Environmental Economics from the University of Massachusetts Amherst. He is a member of the WWF Colombia Board of Directors, the Scientific Board of the Beijer Institute for Ecological Economics in Stockholm, and the Advisory Board of the Center for Behavior and the Environment RARE, USA. He has been a Visiting Professor at Harvard, UCL, the Santa Fe Institute, and Indiana-Bloomington. He obtained the Alejandro Angel Escobar award in the environment and development category in 2009 with his book *Dilemmas de lo Colectivo* and in 2022, he received the Angela Robledo Award from the Colombian Ministry of Science, Technology and Innovation in the category of "Social sciences and human development with equity." His research explores the potential of human groups to solve problems of collective action and cooperation, especially for the self-governed management of ecosystems that support life and the economy.

Fermín Cerezo is IT Engineer. Since 2018, he has served as the Head of Innovation at the Valencia City Council and as the Coordinator of Missions Valencia 2030. With over 15 years of experience, he previously held the position of Director of the Department of Organization, Innovation, and Quality at the Catarroja City Council (1999–2015). In this role, he oversaw technology services, citizen engagement initiatives, public innovation, and organizational development. Throughout his career, he has demonstrated a strong commitment to fostering a professional and competitive public sector. His leadership in modernization, change management, and quality improvement initiatives has been recognized through numerous awards and accolades at the national level.

Ana Escario Chust is a Predoctoral Researcher at the INGENIO (CSIC-UPV) institute from the Polytechnic University of Valencia (UPV) in Spain, specializing in Urban Sustainability Transitions. Her research focuses on participatory governance and innovative methodologies to enhance urban transformation. With a background in Industrial Design, she is interested in creative co-creation methods like design thinking and systemic thinking.

Holding a Master's degree in International Cooperation and Local Development, she brings a global perspective and a strong commitment to addressing urban sustainability challenges from fair and inclusive viewpoints.

John Cleveland serves as Strategic Advisor to the Boston Green Ribbon Commission, USA. He is also President and a Co-founder of the Innovation Network for Communities, a nonprofit focused on social innovation and large-scale change, especially in the ways that communities are responding to climate change – reducing green house gas emissions and strengthening resilience. Prior to founding the Innovation Network for Communities, he served as Vice President of IRN, Inc., a market intelligence firm located in Grand Rapids, Michigan that provided strategic planning, market research, automotive forecasting, and merger and acquisition due diligence to mid-sized manufacturing companies. Prior to joining IRN, he worked as a private consultant; as Director of Continuous Improvement for Grand Rapids Community College; and as Director of the State of Michigan's industrial extension service.

Iván Cuesta is a Postdoctoral Researcher at the Universitat Politecnica de Valencia. He has a background in industrial engineering, with a PhD in African Studies (University of Edinburgh). His latest research explores urban energy transitions and social innovation on the road to net zero. Previously, he researched grassroots innovations in sociotechnical transitions and the political geography of electricity and large-scale infrastructure in Africa. He also teaches geography of development and sustainable development at both Master's and Bachelor's levels.

Débora Domingo is an Architect PhD and Professor at the Universitat Politècnica de València (UPV). Her interests include the methods, means, and impact of architectural research and social consideration in architecture and urban design. Currently, she holds the position of Vice-rector for Sustainable Development of Campus at UPV. She is responsible for planning and launching the university's ecological transition project to achieve carbon neutrality, adapting the actions of the university space to sustainability criteria, and disseminating a culture of environmental awareness.

Duane Elverum is Executive Director and Co-founder of CityStudio Vancouver, as well as a designer and educator. He has taught at the UBC School of Architecture, SFU's Centre for Dialogue, and Emily Carr University of Art and Design. He runs in the mountains, travels widely by van and sailboat, and has undertaken six offshore crossings of the North and South Pacific Oceans. He is a despairing optimist.

Jennifer Houghton is a Senior Lecturer in the Department of Town and Regional Planning at the Durban University of Technology (DUT) in South Africa. She has a Doctorate in Human Geography with research interests in cities, urban development, governance, and quality of life. She spent four years as a Research Associate of the Urban Futures Centre at DUT, focused on urban change in South African cities, with research projects addressing the relationship between urban and economic development processes as well as the implications of global environmental change on flood disasters, lived experiences, and quality of life in Durban. In 2023, she concluded a three-year collaboration with researchers at the University of KwaZulu-Natal and the University of the Western Cape on a National Research Foundation-funded project on the nexus of waste, water, and society in relation to climate change, governance, and South African cities.

Olga Kordas has more than 17 years of experience combining research, teaching, and strategic research and innovation policy and management. She holds the position of Associate Professor in Sustainable Urban Development. Her primary research areas focus on urban data analytics for energy transition and smart and sustainable cities, exploring the role of ICT, electrification, and citizen engagement in enabling sustainable urban development. Since 1 January 2017, she has served as the Director of Viable Cities – the Swedish National Strategic Innovation Program for Smart and Sustainable Cities – a research and innovation funding program running from 2017 to 2030 with a budget of 100 million EUR. Viable Cities is founded on a people-centered holistic approach to sustainable urban development, with digitalization, electrification, and civic engagement as key enablers. It boasts over 90 members representing a quadruple helix collaboration of public authorities, academia, companies, and civil society. Viable Cities stands as one of the pioneering initiatives in Sweden to pilot mission-driven innovation, with the mission "Climate Neutral Cities 2030" with good life for all within planetary boundaries.

Alix Linaker is a social impact specialist and project manager with a decade of experience working at the intersection of various fields including social innovation, education, government, healthcare, and business. She's driven by a deep curiosity about how cross-sectoral and cross-cultural collaboration can be leveraged as a force to tackle and solve systemic social issues.

Bakhetsile Mangena is a Researcher, Academic, and Head of Programme for Human Resource Management and Public Administration from The Independent Institute of Education in South Africa. She obtained her Master's degree in Commerce from the University of KwaZulu-Natal and is currently pursuing a PhD in Town and Regional Planning at the University of Pretoria, with an emphasis on establishing livable cities for higher education. She has presented postgraduate lectures at South African universities including the University of Johannesburg Business School, Mancosa, and the University of KwaZulu-Natal. Bakhetsile, commonly known as BK, headed a team that assisted educational institutions prepare students for the labor market through an employability program using the International Finance Corporation's (part of the World Bank) VITAE 360-degree assessment tool. She took part in a Local Economic Development initiative that received an international award for Best Entrepreneurship and Enterprise Skills in Africa and Best Partnerships for Building Learning Communities in 2014 and 2018, respectively. She also established the Young Researchers Support Project in 2015, allowing young researchers to engage in policy change and implementation projects.

Pablo Aranguiz Mesias is a Chilean community-based scholar who has worked with and for the indigenous Williche people of Chiloé archipelago, Chile, for more than 20 years. He holds a Bachelor's degree in Forestry Engineering from Universidad Mayor, Chile, a Master's degree in Ecosystem Analysis from the University of

Alicante, Spain, and is currently conducting a Doctoral research project at Universitat Politècnica de València, Spain, in the fields of education, youth studies, and just transition to sustainability.

Åsa Minoz is an Innovation policy expert, having worked closely on policy development in Sweden, and on an International basis. Currently, she is Deputy Director of Viable Cities – the Swedish National Strategic Innovation Program for Smart and Sustainable Cities. She is extremely passionate about the potential and power of people as citizens, users, and employees, and in business, third and public sectors to contribute to innovation for a sustainable global society. Some of her key interests revolve around innovation for smart and sustainable cities, climate-neutral cities, innovation in public services, social innovation, social entrepreneurship, and impact investment.

Dionisio Ortiz Miranda is Full Professor at the Department of Economics and Social Sciences at the Universitat Politècnica de València, where he joined in 2000. He holds a degree in Agricultural Engineering from the University of Córdoba (1996) and obtained his PhD from the Department of Agricultural Economics at the same university in 2000. He completed a research stay at the Department of Land Economy at the University of Cambridge, UK, in 2004.

Carla Montagud, PhD in Industrial Engineering from the UPV, is an Associate Professor in the Department of Applied Thermodynamics (DTRA) at the Universitat Politècnica de València (UPV). She serves as the Deputy Director of Sustainable Development at the School of Industrial Engineering (ETSII) of the UPV and is a member of the Board of the University Institute of Research in Energy Engineering (IUIIE), where she has been engaged in research activities for the past 16 years. Additionally, she directs the Urban Energy Transition Chair (CATENERG, https://catenerg.webs.upv.es/en/home-2/) at the UPV. Her research activities are focused on the design, modeling, energy analysis, and techno-economic optimization of complex energy systems. She has been involved in over 25 competitive national and international research and development projects and transfer contracts.

Manuela Navarrete is Ecologist and Biologist from the Pontificia Universidad Javeriana. Currently a Master's student in Applied Economics with an in-depth study of Economics of the Environment and Natural Resources at the Universidad de los Andes. She is specially interested in issues of biodiversity conservation and environmental economics.

Marga Pacis is a Policy Analyst at the City of Vancouver, with a focus on climate policy. Through her work, she aims to contribute to co-creating a built environment that can work in tandem with the natural world, now and for future generations.

Guillermo Palau is Full Professor at the Polytechnic University of Valencia. Holding a degree in Agricultural Engineering and a PhD in Agroforestry Engineering from the same university, he has an extensive research career spanning from engineering to social innovation. With over 20 years of experience leading teams and projects nationally and internationally, he is an expert in applied creativity, innovation, and multidisciplinary team management. His focus lies in systemic innovation, aiding organizations and public institutions in addressing socio-technological transitions. His activities include creativity, design thinking, system analysis, working with future scenarios, and circular economy. He has participated in more than 20 national and international research and transfer projects and contracts.

Carla Panyella is Tourism Administration Professional with a Master's in International Relations from the Pompeu Fabra University, the University of Barcelona, and the Autonomous University of Barcelona, and a Master's in Development Practice from the Universidad de los Andes. She was part of the work team of the SCALA Observatory of the School of Management of Universidad de los Andes as Head of Alliances and Research and worked as a project coordinator at a Colombian NGO. She seeks to develop professionally in the coordination and formulation of projects that contribute to the economic, environmental, and social development of Latin America and the Caribbean through science and technology diplomacy.

Mónica Pinilla-Roncancio is Physiotherapist from the Universidad del Rosario, with a Master's degree in Economics from the same university and a Master's degree in Health Economics from Erasmus University in Rotterdam, the Netherlands. She finished her PhD in Social Policy in 2015 at the University of Birmingham, UK. Between 2016 and 2018, she was a Postdoctoral Researcher at the School of Medicine of the Universidad de los Andes. Currently, she works as an Assistant Professor at the School of Medicine and is the Deputy Director of the Center for Sustainable Development Goals for Latin America and the Caribbean. She has been a Research Associate at the Oxford Poverty and Human Development Initiative since 2015, from 2019 to 2021 she was the Director of Measurement and Policy at the same research center. Her main research topics are disability, poverty, health economics, and inequality. She has experience working with countries in Latin America and the Caribbean, Africa, and Asia.

Harald Rohracher is Professor of Technology and Social Change at Linköping University. He has been Co-founder and Director of the Inter-University Research Centre for Technology, Work and Culture (IFZ), Graz, Austria (1999–2007), Joseph A. Schumpeter Fellow at Harvard University (2009–2010), and Simon Visiting Professor at Manchester University (2013). He has many years of research experience in the field of sustainability transitions, transformative innovation policy, governance of socio-technical change, urban low-carbon transitions, and more recently also on questions of evaluation of mission-oriented programs and the concept of just transitions. Until recently he has been Associate Editor of the journal Environmental Innovations and Societal Transitions. His recent publications include "Mission incomplete: Layered practices of monitoring and evaluation in Swedish transformative innovation policy," Science and Public Policy, 2023 (together with Lars Coenen and Olga Kordas).

Nayla Saniour is trained as an architect and works at the Center itdUPM of the Technical University of Madrid as a Project Coordinator and Facilitator of multi-stakeholder collaborations for sustainable transitions. She received her Bachelor's degree in Architecture from the American University of Beirut, and her Master's in Strategies and Technologies for Development from the Technical University of Madrid.

Azanta Thakur Administrative Coordinator and Project Manager for the Boston Green Ribbon Commission, USA. She has been deeply engaged in climate work in Boston since graduating from Boston University in 2020 and brings a variety of administrative, management, and organizational skills to her role at GRC, including event planning, social media management, communications and marketing, and diversity and justice. She received her Bachelor's degree in Health Science and Environmental Analysis and Policy from Boston University and is currently pursuing her Master's in Public Health from the University of South Florida. In her free time, she loves trying new recipes and finding new stories to consume.

Oksana Udovyk is a Marie-Curie Postdoctoral Researcher at Universitat Politècnica de València, INGENIO [CSIC-UPV]. She obtained her Bachelor's degree in Natural Sciences from the National University of Kyiv-Mohyla Academy, Ukraine, a Master's degree in Sustainable Development from Linköping University, Sweden, and a PhD in Environmental Governance from Linköping and Södertörn Universities, Sweden. Her current research interests focus on urban transformations and recovery efforts in the European Union and Ukraine.

www.ingramcontent.com/pod-product-compliance
Lightning Source LLC
Chambersburg PA
CBHW052057230426
43662CB00037B/1987